Maire Mullarney
Argues about Language

Maire Mullarney
Argues about Language

ARLEN
HOUSE

ISBN 1–903631–47–5 *paperback*

First published by Arlen House in May 2004

Arlen House
PO Box 222
Galway
Ireland

42 Grange Abbey Road
Baldoyle
Dublin 13

arlenhouse@ireland.com
www.arlenhouse.com

Typesetting: Arlen House
Printed by: ColourBooks, Baldoyle, Dublin 13

Cover by Rebecca Zak

TALKING ABOUT LANGUAGE

Before you read any of this collection you should understand that these pages were written during about twenty years. All but one were written in response to a Call for Papers, for contributions to a planned conference or symposium about some aspects of language. This meant that speakers would be talking to other speakers, not to an audience who might have assembled in order to listen.

Even though I soon recognised that there was practically no chance that questions might lead to any practical interest in an inter-people language I offered papers when the subjects listed gave me an opening. I wanted people involved in linguistics to know that Esperanto is by no means dead.

Now, rather unexpectedly, the opportunity to have a selection published by Arlen House (which published my first book, *Anything School Can Do, YOU Can Do Better)* means that readers who are not dashing off to give their own paper may quietly read several overlapping arguments and even join an ever-increasing flow of European and world-wide activity.

Dip in anywhere; there is no sequence. I suggest, though, that *Experientia docet: simultaneous translation not the answer*, given in the Spanish Department of the University of Amsterdam to a Colloquium on *Las lenguas de la Europa*

Communitaria, may paint a background. I was delighted by a footnote to printed text: *Nota de los editores: Dado lo especial del artículo y las circunstancias de su escritora, el comite cientifico de Coloquio ha dado el visto bueno para su publicación.*

Maire Mullarney, Dublin, April 2004

WHAT HARM ARE WE DOING?

Is it possible that while we go
around the world warning and advising,
our exhaust is leaving a lethal trail?

Do the words. 'Typhoid Mary' ring a bell? Our own Dr. Jim Deeny was a pioneer in tracing 'carriers' who, while seemingly healthy, bring a specific illness, whether typhoid or TB wherever they go. When he retired from the World Health Organization he set up in his home town the Tagoat Experience, a local answer to unemployment which was of one mind with Feasta. His autobiography *To Cure and to Care* deserves to be read. However, it is not his book that I am writing about, but two others, *Translation and Globalization* by Michael Cronin and *English-Only Europe?* by Robert Phillipson, both published by Routledge in 2003.

In the latter Phillipson methodically describes a state of affairs with which I am familiar through e-mail, but which is shrouded from the Irish public. Information about global warming, GM plants, the movement of manufacturing to low-wage economies, for example, is available to anyone even half-interested, though our government seems unconcerned. Phillipson, who is Research Professsor in the Dept. of English in Copenhagen Business School, asks significant questions in a different field. How does English as the key language of globalization impact on economic, cultural and educational policies in continental Europe? Do procedures followed in conducting EU affairs give native speakers of the 'top' languages, particularly English and French, unfair advantages, and, if so, what can be done to remedy the problem?

That EU procedures are unfair is demonstrated by the complaint made in May 2002 to the EU Ombudsman about job ads requiring 'English mother-tongue or equivalent'. The Commission apologised, but the practice continues, slightly modified. The majority of European students who take advantage of the SOCRATES exchange programme use it to improve their English. Ministers in Greece and Denmark have proposed that English be adopted as the 'second official language', causing shock waves. Indeed, several EU countries have active voluntary organizations designed to protect their own languages while recognising the specific threat of 'world English'. The Polish and Hungarian governments have legislated to restrict the spread of English, but Phillipson argues that many governments allow responsibility for language to be spread over too many different departments.

A Japanese communications scholar reports that native speakers of Japanese, whether ambassadors, scholars or business people, experience that they simply have fewer rights than speakers of English in most contexts of international communication. Japanese culture is now so strongly influenced by the west that the

Japanese have become obsessed by 'Anglomania' and the need to learn English, though they are not completely successful at doing so. English is taught ever earlier in the school system, and pre-school mothers are now more proud of their children being able to speak English than Japanese. Taiwan has set up a massive recruitment programme for 'native speakers of English' to teach it in all schools.

Phillipson, in a chapter discussing global trends in language policy, states that it was the triumphant American state that fashioned the present 'global economy' at Bretton Woods in 1944, so that its military and corporate arms would have unlimited access to minerals, oil, markets and cheap labour. In 1948 George Kennan, the State Department's senior planner, wrote:

> We have 50 per cent of the world's wealth, but only 6.3 per cent of its population. In this situation, our real job in the coming period is to devise a pattern of relationships which permit us to maintain this position of disparity. To do so, we have to dispense with all sentimentality ... we should cease thinking about human rights, the raising of living standards and democratisation.

The World Bank and the International Monetary Fund were invented to implement this strategy. Phillipson demonstrates that English is an integral dimension of this globalizaton project, showing that the process of establishing US global hegemony was supported by the expenditure of large amounts of government and private foundation funds in the period 1950–1970.

> British and American policy was coordinated in the pioneer phase of creating the academic infrastructure, institutions and professionalism that would ensure that native speaker expertise was considered relevant worldwide.

English-Only Europe? is admirably planned and laid out, with examples of confusion in legal terminology or of the different implications of 'our daily bread' arranged in boxes for easy comparison.

One such Box (5.2) that demonstrates international communication shows that when British journalists interview non-native speakers of English they make few if any allowances for the fact that those interviewed are speaking in a foreign language. An example is taken from an interview in December 2001 when a newly appointed Danish Foreign Minister was being questioned for BBC World. The BBC journalist frequently interrupted the Minister and made many statements ending in a tag question (it's like this isnt it?), with falling intonation which is used in standard English when agreement by the interlocutor is expected. For example, the initial question involved a series of statements, ending up with 'Isn't that rather disingenuous?'

> ... The journalist said that she (a Danish MP) let the cat out of the bag. This term was not

> understood, providing a clear instance of ineffective communication caused by a native speaker. The journalist reformulated the question, and asked whether the Minister agreed with what the MP had said, to which he replied that he did not. The journalist then asked whether the MP was speaking out of turn, meaning without authority to do so. The Minister paused, and stated that she was speaking out of tune ...

The interview as a whole was generally regarded as having shown the Minister making a complete fool of himself. The programme roused so much interest that it was shown several times on Danish television. Danish journalists had a field day commenting on the Minister's English. None raised the question of whether the communicative inequality, the asymmetrical communication, and the insensitive native speaker language was defensible. When reading this one should remember that Phillipson lives and works in Denmark, normally using three languages.

Earlier in this paper I said that the book describes a state of affairs with which I am familiar through the internet. I was pleased to recognise, on p. 123, a quotation from an instruction given by the EU Commission to the Czech Republic:

> 1 Any communication between the Commission and the Czech Republic related to the agreement shall be in English.
>
> 2 The Czech republic shall ensure that ... relevant national legislation, written

> procedures manuals, guidelines ... standard documents and forms shall be available in English, the Czech Republic shall provide texts in English expeditiously following a request from the commission.

After being alerted originally to this instruction. I had copied the full text and circulated it, in several colours, under the heading: 'As a European, are you content with this instruction?' My copy included the instruction that the translation should be 'at its own expense'. I sent it to various Ministers and TDs; I even took the opportunity to put it into the pocket of Pat Cox, MEP.

How had I come to see it? Through a regular internet communications from the Europa Esperanto-Unio. In this case the text was given in English.

Phillipson's fmal chapter is entitled 'Towards equitable communication'. Here he draws attention to the inherent difficulties of writing and pronouncing English. He reports his own experience at two international conferences, one in Hong Kong on Language Rights, conducted entirely in English; when a South African participant asked why the many Asians who had difficulty expressing themselves in English accepted this the answer was that the organisers had not given the matter any thought and the participants from all over Asia were too polite to protest. His second experience, a couple of weeks later, was a symposium during an Esperanto congress in Prague:

> It was amazing to experience participants from all over the world communicating confidently in a shared international language, among them many Asians who manifestly were at no disadvantage. As this event was my first experience of Esperanto in action (with interpretation provided for us non-Esperantists), it was a vivid and memorable way of seeing that it is not merely Utopian ...

The last couple of pages ask whether there might be a language better suited to equality in communication. He says that there is a tendency for those not familiar with Esperanto to reject it without seriously investigating whether it might provide a more efficient and equitable solution to some problems of international communication, and contribute to making foreign language learning in schools more effective. 'A tendency to reject' is a mild description of the behaviour of English-language media and politicians.

There follows a concise account of the origin of the language, of its unanimous acceptance by the Assembly of the League of Nations, of fierce French resistance and of subsequent attempts by an organisation which has no financial resources to influence language policy in international organisations. While the French authorities had merely resisted this pacifist language, Hitler and Stalin in turn endeavoured to liquidate its speakers.

English-Only Europe? gives a clear, very readable account of a state of affairs which I suspect must be surprising to Irish readers. *Translation and Globalization* by Michael Cronin, Dean of the Joint Faculty of Humanities at Dublin City University is also decidedly readable (in Esperanto, 'leginda', deserving to be read) and surprising in quite a different way. Cronin ranges through continents, millennia and languages, touching base in Ireland from time to time. In his introduction he says that his study attempts to understand the specific role of translation at this particular moment in time, to show to those outside the discipline (and within it, too, of course) that translation deals with questions which are of real importance for the past, present and future of humanity. The most cursory survey of the literature in political science, sociology and cultural studies would suggest that at present, nobody really is listening.

A world economy is nothing new; the history of empires has shown us that capital accumulation proceeding throughout the world has been with us for a long time. A global economy is something different; it is an economy with the capacity to work as a unit in real time on a planetary scale. This capacity is the fruit of the astonishingly rapid developments of information technology which has seen us shift from a technology based on cheap inputs of energy to one predominantly based on cheap inputs of information.

Cheap inputs: a little further we meet the dismay of Bill Gates at the mounting cost of 'localization' of Microsoft products. For him it was 'just a linguistic process'. For Cronin:

> what is being contested here is not so much the use of the term 'localization' to describe a set of activities in the software industry as the manner in which the term is used to make invisible and depoliticize translation in the modem world.

Implicit here is not that translation would disappear but that it would be transferred … entirely carried out by non-English speakers who must translate themselves into English, so rendering themselves invisible in much the same way as the separate linguistic loyalties (Scots, Welsh, Irish) of the footsoldiers in Henry V are concealed by the unitary English of Shakespeare's play.

But somehow we find ourselves going underground. Darwin's last work, published in 1881, the year before he died, was entitled *The Formation of Vegetable Mould through the Action of Worms, with Observations on their Habits*. Here he demonstrated that they are prodigiously active creatures, that through their continuous digestion of the soil worms were effectively breaking it up, making it available for new growth. In addition, because worms cannot swallow coarse particles like lime or pottery or bones, they cover them with fine earth, thus protecting them from exposure. Darwin showed how human agriculture was doomed without the concealed labour of the lowly, hidden and marginalized. Moving from the natural ecosystem to the cultural ecosystem, it is time cultural critics turned their eyes to what lies beneath the ground of cultures, the soil which nourishes their continued vitality. Descending from heaven to earth, we find in countless recorded cultures the invisible, unrecorded work of the legions of translators working on the planet.

Cronin looks back to the Sumerian-Eblaite vocabularies inscribed on clay tablets, estimated by archeologists to be 4,500 years old, then to the library of Alexandria, which was to contain all the books of the known world. It was not enough that they be collected. They must also be translated if Ptolemy's scholars were to extract any benefit from them. He gives an account also of the circumstances under which 72 translators, in a mansion built by the seashore, magnificently appointed, translate the books of the the Hebrew Bible into Greek.

The Septuagint appears again in an account of Bedell's translation of the Bible into Irish Gaelic, when he used controls. But this is still translation as we used to know it. Later chapters tell of the enormous pressures placed on translators by modern technology. 'The shift from the industrial to the informational society implies at one level the breaching of manageable limits in volume growth for human translators'. The human processing of human texts in time is increasingly annulled by the technology of delivery, so that the time values are those of the machine, not of the human being.

And delivery constraints do not now allow me to quote Dean Swift's sharp letter, in French, to the French translator of Gulliver, or look at the problems of post-colonial translation or observe that translators are, like Mad Sweeney, creatures of the air, haunted by the restlessness and unquiet of their age. But what I can do is explain why I undertook to write such an inadequate review of a book overflowing with knowledge of literature, language and technology.

I wanted to ask a serious question.

How can its author know so much and yet not know that there is such a language as Esperanto, which enables translators to translate from their mother tongue, no matter how small the minority who share it, into their own creative, flexible second language and make the content available to all the world?

This is a question Umberto Eco asked, when researching *La ricerca della lingua perfetta nella cultura europea* 'how could I not have known about it?'

The theme of this paper is the neglect of the wide and varied competence of the international planned language, Esperanto, especially of its unique role in relation to other languages. It is agreeable to be able to refer to some improvements in this matter which have occurred in the meantime.

Not that there has been any significant change in the context of the European Union. Speaking at a conference in 1993 I began by saying that it is *understandable* that EU officials should look *coldly* on 'a second language for everyone' an accessible language, a language free from ambiguity, one that could save half the budget of the EU.

My intention was to elicit surprise. Surely any adminstration would prefer to save half its budget, surely it is normally preferable to avoid ambiguity? Esperanto users from many countries, including officials of the Council of Europe, were naive enough to think so; they prepared these arguments, with detailed costings, and expected them to be persuasive. It was only when I spoke to an Irishman, experienced in making applications for EU grants, that I learnt how ingenuous we were. He explained that each member state is more concerned to see as many as possible of its citizens employed as translators, secretaries or simply in the support system.

Well, we'll see whether three or five or ten additional countries make any difference.

Signs of Spring

Recognition in Rome

I had wished to use the Roman Catholic Church as another example, as neglect by this church is peculiarly unaccountable. Books have been written about it both in Polish and Esperanto (Korytkowski 1976). In English I discussed the matter in the journal *Language Problems and Language Planning*. It is surely remarkable that a world-wide organisation in which responsible persons had a common language for the last sixteen hundred years should inadvertently allow this means of communication to slip away because of a decision (by the Vatican Council in 1966) to use more accessible languages for worship. The result has been that when bishops assemble for a Synod they have at once to dis-assemble into language groups. In March 1994 the African Synod had to divide into Anglophone and Francophone groupings. This should not have been necessary; quite a few bishops speak Esperanto. Most bishops must be old enough to have used Latin during their seminary studies; compared with Latin, Esperanto is a doddle.

But here we have signs of a thaw. Pope John Paul II uses a great many languages for traditional papal Easter greetings, now widely broadcast. The Catholic Esperanto (IKUE) association has been trying for years to persuade him to include that language, in which he is perfectly competent. He is also well known to be stubborn. However, on this he changed his mind; last Easter, the 3 April, his 56th and second-last language was Esperanto: 'Feliĉan Paskon en Kristo resurektinta'. And last may not be least, since the last of all was the Pope's mother-tongue, Polish.

The Radical Party claims the credit for persuading him; I wonder could he have been influenced by Umberto Eco's book, *The Search for the Perfect Language,* published to much acclaim in 1995.

Education

At the same time the Italian Ministry for Education released the report of a Commission which recommended that Esperanto be introduced in primary schools, since it had been found to give to children who learn it significant advantages in acquiring further languages.

International goodwill

A little earlier another international body, UNESCO, passed its third favourable resolution. It warmly recommends to Non-Governmental Organisations that they should take advantage of this accessible, neutral language. 'Do as I say, don't do as I do'.

And on 12 April 1994 the 32-nation Council of Europe elected as Secretary General for the next five years Daniel Tarschys, from Sweden; he taught himself Esperanto as a boy; this prompted him to interest himself in international affairs and to learn a number of other languages also.

Hungary has appointed as Ambassador to the Russian Federation Gyorgy Namovfsky, formerly editor of an Esperanto journal *Planlingvistiko* as well as an official of the UN. He says he takes every opportunity to support the language but realises that to flourish as it should it needs money.

International PEN compared with these organisations is a modest affair, but it can give a testimony of its own. During its annual congress in Santiago de Compostela in October 1993 it accepted an Esperanto section into membership. I am especially pleased about this because, by coincidence, Irish PEN around the same time invited me to apply for membership. I can therefore insist both from the approval of a body concerned only with literary merit and from my own experience as a writer that Esperanto is very far from being a mere flat impersonal means to convey bald facts. Writing in Esperanto is creative, expressive and enjoyable in a way difficult to make clear to those not acquainted with the language.

A Literary Language

I sometimes try to explain that native speakers of English who wish to write acceptably have to skip over 'idiom chunks' to find fresh expression in a way that is just the reverse of the way one has to leap rapidly from one semi-solid tussock to another when making one's way over a bog. In contrast, writing in Esperanto is more like walking freely over open heath or mountainside, finding flowers never seen before.

Roget's Vision

And that little excursion gives me an untimely excuse to mention Roget's *Thesaurus of English Words and Phrases*, generally acknowledged to be indispensable to writers and translators. My Everyman edition provides Peter Roget's original introduction at the end of the volume. Here we can read how the man who had the vision and competence to supply, with respect to the English language,

> a desideratum hitherto unsupplied in any language; namely, a collection of the words it contains and the idiomatic combinations peculiar to it, arranged, not in alphabetical order, as they are in a dictionary, but according to the ideas which they express ...thoughts about the search for a universal language.

In the final paragraphs of his introduction Roget, a man who had made such a thorough study of the uses of English, looks forward to the realization of: 'that splendid aspiration of philanthropists – the establishment of a Universal Language'. The probable result of the construction of such a language would be, he writes, 'its eventual adoption by every civilized nation'.

The initiator of Esperanto

Roget wrote this introduction in 1852. He died in 1869, when Lazarus Ludovic Zamenhof was aged ten, already striving to find the design for a language that would allow mutual understanding between all peoples and banish violence together with delusions of superiority. I do not think it probable that Roget's book found its way to Poland; the discussion of affixes and opposites would have been very helpful to young Zamenhof, who published his First Book, *Unua Libro*, eighteen years later, in 1887.

The Gene Pool

To return to the European Union: Its left hand makes regulations for the preservation of natural beauty. Its right hand, however, favouring 'the market economy' allows sale of only a restricted set of seed varieties. To counter these regulations, a network of gardeners and botanists collect and grow and preserve as many existing varieties as possible. Similarly, the EU in principle holds that every citizen should be enabled to speak their own language in the Parliament and elsewhere, but can provide only for the dominant language of each member state and in practice allows English to be 'first among equals'.

In the wider world destruction of rainforest and the spread of single crops for the market, are destroying plant and insect species at a horrifying rate. Botanists and entomologists struggle to capture even their traces.

But students of language – the word 'linguist' is hardly adequate, in Esperanto one can distinguish between lingvistoj and lingvistikistoj – also try to capture remnants of disappearing languages. They categorise them. Topic? VSO? They sift for Universal Grammar. What do they do to help threatened languages survive? A Hungarian group are compiling a Red Book of Endangered Languages but they are doing so by means of Esperanto, which could, if supported, provide the best protection.

The Threat

Professor John Honey, a professor of TEFL, the teaching of English as a Foreign Language, stated firmly and publicly in 1989 that English is killing one language a week worldwide, while of the millions who try to learn English the greater number fail. He was content; English is the world language; it's what people want.

Is it what linguists want? I know that there are those who hold that it is not proper to interfere; the scientific attitude is simply to observe. But in fact there is endless destructive interference. If Honey is correct, there will be nothing left to study except pidgins and creoles.

A Shield

My impression is that Anglo-American speaking linguists look on Esperanto as beneath serious notice. The fact that anyone of average intelligence can, at almost any age, in a relatively short time, learn to write and speak it correctly must indeed be off-putting to those who seek complexity in the same spirit as climbers seek perpendicular mountains. Others choose minutely to observe the inherited quirks of English. Many, I think, believe it is enough to observe, that the notion of correctness is an imposition on language.

In reply I would say that for one young person to design a structure which would surpass in accessability, clarity and creativity a thousand other projects should be seen as a superb achievement in the domain of language. Others find it worthy of study; it is in Japan that Zamenhof's complete works have been collected and published. Perhaps I should not take it for granted that everyone understands that young Zamenhofs aim was only to protect, never to replace existing languages; to provide 'a second language for everyone'.

The Perfect Language

I had not expected to have any need to say this. I was aware that Umberto Eco's new book, *La ricerca della lingua perfetta* had been published in Italy and had been warmly received; that German, Spanish, French and English translations were subsequently to be published. I ordered the

English version, *The Perfect Language,* which was to be published by Blackwell, eventually appearing in March 1995.

The book is based on a lecture series, The Search for the Perfect Language, given in the College de France. While preparing his lectures Eco discovered Esperanto and was astonished that he had not known about earlier. All I know yet is that the Italian Esperanto association is over the moon about it. But it might turn out that a professor of semiotics who writes novels would not be considered an authority. Perhaps a recent comment from Claude Hagège may have more weight. He is reported to have said that Esperanto may be considered, according to its structure, as one of the great languages of Europe and that, among proposed solutions to the language problem, it has the serious advantage that, unlike any other language with a possibly serious role in Europe, it neither supports nor follows any political or national obligations.

This testimony is another indication of a return of the tide favouring Esperanto. I heard Hagège give a plenary lecture in the Sorbonne during a conference years ago; he made a passing polite reference to Zamenhof; nothing like this.

Terminology

First hand

I shall conclude by reference to another speaker whom I heard in Warsaw in 1987. The

Director of the Terminology Sector of the UN translation service Dr. Nigel Cassar, described the intense pressure under which his Section worked and said that he was convinced that Esperanto could meet all needs of communication and precision. He begged his hearers to presuade their national governments to lobby for the language.

It is not surprising that Dr. Cassar should find it appropriate to his work. The science of Terminology was initiated by Wüster and Drezen, because of their experience as competent users of Esperanto. Indeed, their individual experiences in this matter have relevance. E. K. Drezen, in the Soviet Union, from 1932 onwards concentrated on research into the normalization of technical terms. He helped to popularise in his country the pioneer work in this field, published in 1931 by the Austrian terminologist Eugen Wuster, who – an esperantist since his youth – argued in favour of wide use of Esperanto for international normalization of technical terms, especially in electronics. As president of the terminology section of the Normalization Committee of the USSR, Drezen worked out a project for establishing an international code based on the main principles of Esperanto. The Committee presented this report in September 1934 to ISA (International Federation of National Normalization Associations) who unanimously accepted it and commissioned the Soviet Committee to continue the research. I found this information in *La Dangera Lingvo,* a 500-page book documenting persecution of users of Esperanto by dictatorial regimes, especially by direction of Hitler and Stalin, who had Drezen executed.

In Europe we hear of the 'democratic deficit'. Will there be any democratic fall-out from the following address to electors published before a previous election in the newspapers of record in the EU countries?

> Electors of Europe!
>
> Is anyone prepared to tackle the trammels of language? The effect of the official policy of multilingualism is simply to force us to try to learn English but never to master it. This policy leaves us always unsure, always undignified. The LINGUA programme is no solution. How should a Dane who speaks German and English talk to a Greek who chose to learn Italian and French?
>
> The institutions of the European Union translate every day 3.6 million words. Every single word costs 2 French Francs, about 25 Irish pence. So much for concern about 'Poverty and Exclusion'.
>
> Is the problem insoluble? It is not. There is an inexpensive, democratic, psychologically acceptable solution, long proposed, more recently by Umberto Eco in his book *The Search for the Perfect Language* and by Claude Piron in *Le defi des langues*. Comparisons between this and competing solutions (use of English, simultaneous interpreting, etc.) demonstrate that Esperanto is much the most satisfactory. Those who reject this have never compared the various solutions in practice, in real life, so speak without authority.

As for the suggestion that Esperanto is a handicap in respect of learning other languages, this is altogether the reverse of the truth; it has been found over and over again, in many countries, to encourage confidence and early competence in foreign languages – not to speak of competence in the mother tongue.

Let us demand the solution which offers the most protection and respect to our rich variety of cultures. Let us give our votes in this European election to those candidates who show that they are aware of the language problem and who reject the unjust discrimination against Esperanto.

Experemtia Docet: Simultaneous Translation is not the Solution

I would like to warn readers that this paper is rather unusual. I have heard and read a good many papers given at language seminars, colloquiums and conferences. I have, then, encountered papers discussing the teaching of a second language, learning at various ages, by immersion, by self-instruction; the effects of contact, dialects, creoles, pidgins; special features of 'foreigner talk', of women's and men's speech patterns, and many, many more topics, of which everyone reading this could make a list. I have given some myself. It is the norm for such papers to refer to what others have written on the same topic and to list the references. The first person singular is to be avoided.

I have yet to find reflection on conferences themselves, linguistic conferences and other conferences, the experience of listening to one language, of listening to several, of listening to simultaneous translation, of using whispered translation, of exhaustion, of incomprehension, of various forms of frustration. My experience is that such frustration is endemic in the struggle with languages in the European Union and therefore I think it relevant to recount some of that experience. I am Irish. At home I have always spoken English. I have no reason to believe that any of my great grandparents were Irish speakers.

Conference problems

My first international conference, over thirty years ago, had deficiencies which I have met many times since then. I had been living at home, bringing up our eleven children. The Catholic Church's ban on contraception had come into question. My husband and I were rather better informed on moral theology that the average lay person. I joined a few interested doctors in setting up Ireland's first Family Planning centre and soon found myself a delegate to the Europe Region meeting of International Planned Parenthood. About eighty people took part, representing forty countries – Turkey had delegates, as well as many countries from the eastern side of the Iron Curtain. There was a flow of extremely interesting information, in a single language, English. I was especially impressed by a Polish philosopher who urged that children in their first years in school should be taught that to be a mother or a father was a serious, responsible occupation. Unfortunately, neither his command of English idiom nor his pronunciation were adequate to the excellence of his contribution. We broke up into several workshops for discussion. Even though it was my first time to take part, it was a matter of course that, as a native speaker of English, I should be rapporteur for my group. I also had to interpret, using Spanish, a discussion between a Welsh doctor and a Portuguese priest.

Recently I had a similar experience. BIEN, the Basic Income European Network, had a conference in Vienna, with some translation for plenary sessions, but not for workshops. A Spanish economist brought to a workshop copies in Spanish of a very interesting paper, with an abstract in variable English. This he read. When people asked questions in English he endeavoured to answer, but my impression was that few realised the value of his contribution. Indeed, I have found myself on the other side of the fence, but that must wait until it is time to talk of simultaneous translation.

Before that, I should mention the most primitive solution: sentence-by-sentence translation, when the speaker pauses after each sentence and, according to the number of languages required, volunteers in different parts of the room interpret for those around them as quietly as they can. Never quietly enough. Nothing could be less satisfactory. I can understand why, when technology began to make simultaneous translation possible, it seemed heaven-sent.

The use of French and English has a long tradition behind it and is said to be the way of life of the United Nations. It serves well enough provided that most people taking part understand both languages, even if they prefer to avoid speaking one of them. It may be difficult to agree a final document which combines the results of discussions in the two languages. This has been known to take the whole night, after the conclusion of the conference.

My experience during four years as Irish delegate to the European Co-ordination of Green Parties was interesting. (I had been involved in setting up the Irish Green Party). At first the Co-ordination had representatives from only five or six countries. We would usually meet for two days every three months. On one day we would have simultaneous translation of English and French, the translators being professionals who worked for us as volunteers. As I suppose everyone knows, simultaneous translation is too tiring to be continued for more than fifteen minutes, so the two who translate English into French take over one from the other at that interval, as do the other team who translate from French into English. On the second day we would continue our discussions without help, in English; I noticed that some people who had had plenty to say in French tended to remain silent. As one of the two or three native speakers of English, I would be expected to record the minutes. All meetings were chaired by an English woman or a Swedish delegate who spoke English really well.

As time went on, Green parties were founded in different countries and it was impossible to find as many volunteer translators as we needed. It must be remembered that the addition of German to the service required, in theory, four more for German-English and another four for French to and from German. I remember the great difficulty a French interpreter experienced when a Portuguese woman gave her report in the best French she could manage. The interpreter could not understand what was said and had to abandon her task and leave it to the Greens to puzzle out something between them.

This is a well known hazard of simultaneous translation. During another conference in Firenze, in Italy, when BIEN had the facilities of the European University, I had a conversation with an Italian translator. She told me that her father was Italian and her mother English, so she felt equally at home in both languages. Normally interpreters listen to languages they have learnt and express the meaning in their own mother-tongue. For this woman it was as easy to speak English while hearing Italian as to speak in Italian while listening to English. Her problem was, how to cope with an Italian speaking what he supposed was English, but which was littered with Italian constructions. She said that in effect her brain could not decide which language it was processing, so was at a loss to know which set of words should emerge. She found this extremly stressful.

I am concerned to add that even when one has not the responsibility for reproduction, it is usually rather disagreeable to listen for twenty minutes or half an hour to a non-native speaker give a talk, in English. I am reminded of a French environmental scientist who spoke in Dublin to an EU conference on Environmental Diversity. Our then Prime Minister, Garret Fitzgerald, said it was probably the most significant conference he had ever attended. I was there as a journalist and I did find it exciting, but what I most remember is how this speaker read his paper, continually putting stress where an English speaker would not, and with pronunciation that made some words unrecognisable. When it was time for questions, delegates asked in one of the available languages and the speaker replied in clear and agreeable French.

Finding a Solution

I have just said that I suppose everyone knows how pairs of professional interpreters share the task, but I realise that it quite probable that some people present take part only in linguistic seminars, where translation is not expected. Now my first experience of a language-oriented world-congress was AILA 84, in Brussels. I must explain that in about 1980 I had first happened to encounter, in the Esperanto-Museo in Vienna, this planned language and found it alluring. The next year I joined a small ecumenical congress, found that, with a dictionary in my bag, I could become involved in discussions about anything under the sun, from unemployment to the Holy Trinity. To a comparison of their respective Finno-Ugaritic languages by a Finnish woman and a Hungarian priest during breakfast I could only listen

In 1982 the Esperanto Universala Kongreso was held in Antwerp, and I enjoyed that. Subsequently I took part in several of these Congresses, in Hungary, Norway, China, with seven thousand others in Warsaw, the Centenary Congress. I have described these, and what follows here, in my book *Esperanto for Hope*, (republished as *Everyone's Own Language)*. And there I have space to explain that the meetings of the Komitato, representatives from fifty or sixty countries, function smoothly, rapidly, with no interpreters and perfect comprehension.

When in 1983 it was suggested that I should study for a graduate diploma in theoretical linguistics in Trinity College, Dublin, this seemed an excellent way to find out whether Esperanto was as remarkable as I had come to suppose. A 'call for papers' for AILA 84 arrived in the post. When I read it the closing date had already passed, but the theme was 'International Communication' or something of the sort. I sent off an abstract in which I asserted that English was not a suitable language for international communication. To my surprise it was accepted. And the paper I wrote opened with the words, in Esperanto:

> Do not be surprised if the interpreters remain silent. In a moment I shall repeat what I am saying in French and then in English. If most of you could understand what I am saying now, there would be no need for me to speak.

It was a further surprise for me that there were no interpreters. But there was an active group of Esperanto-speakers. A book I had written dealing with reading acquisition had just been published and provoked an amount of interest. I had a lovely time. And nothing that I heard or saw persuaded me that English was perfectly satisfactory. There is not time to list here the variety of errors that I heard in papers given by non-native speakers using English; I noted one, from Sweden, who spoke the language really well. There may have been others whom I did not hear. I was struck by the incorrect English used on notice boards. I was accustomed to seeing and noting very amusing errors in other environments – but this was congress of linguists! My prize example of the problem was one of the plenary lectures. An Indian professor spoke at length about the mother-tongue. He spoke in English. Afterwards I went to have a cup of coffee and was joined by a gentleman whom I had not met (He was tall, suntanned, and wore an elegant white suit). Straight away he asked me in Esperanto whether I had understood the lecture we had just heard. I replied that I knew it was about the mother-tongue but I had no idea what had been said about it. 'Ah', he replied 'then you were at least more fortunate that the two Americans with whom I was sitting. They had no idea at all of what it might be about'.

Simultaneous Translation

So much for my first linguistic congress. Now I would like to say something more about simultaneous translation. In the Green meetings which I have mentioned we usually sat in a hollow square, so that one knew who was the speaker, even if the interpreter changed with his or her partner, so that the voice one was hearing changed.

This was also the case during large conferences, when translation of a single speech would be heard spoken by alternating voices, but there would be no doubt about the prime source, the speaker at the speaker's desk.

Here is the really unsatisfactory aspect of this technological support system. When the Green numbers had increased we sometimes had the use of meeting rooms in the European Parliament buildings, with parliamentary interpreters. We would be seated in several rows of desks. If one relied on the hearing apparatus, the headphone, one would hear words in the language to which one had turned the indicator, but one might easily be at a loss to know who was speaking, and in which language – unless the speaker was using one's chosen language, in which case one would hear her or his voice directly. If a discussion should develop, one would at least hear the questions, arguments, in the voice of one (or both) of the interpreters. But sometimes it could even happen that an argument would be conducted between two people speaking the same language, neither of whom the headphoned listener could identify. I can remember turning around, looking every way, to see if I could find out who was speaking.

Duel in the Dark

Green and allied parties arranged a two-day session in the Parliament building, with full teams of parliamentary interpreters to debate Basic

Income. [Several Green Parties believe that the time has come to change the various systems of Social Welfare, which are based on the notion that employment is the normal way to gain an income and that State money should be given only to people who are not employed, given, therefore on condition that they are not earning anything. This is not the place to explain why some competent people observe that this condition means that unemployed people cannot reasonably take jobs that do not pay well, well enough to replace the various supports they would have to relinquish. The alternative proposal is an Unconditional Individual Basic Income/*Allocation Universelle* which would permit recipients to work and earn. The purpose of the session was to discuss this proposal, not only among Greens, but with other politicians as well].

It was a worth while discussion but what I want to report about it is that during a debate between one or two Italian delegates and one of the proposers of Basic Income I removed my headphones from time to time and recognised that the Italians were talking about something entirely different, a Minimum Wage, but translation did not allow this to become clear, I must emphasize that the Basic Income concept is of an income not related to work or occupation – just like an inherited income – while a minimum wage is concerned only with how much a worker is paid for working. You will see this was like a duel with the opponents in two different rooms.

I wrote earlier that I have found myself misunderstood. This was during an EU funded conference on Poverty and Exclusion, in Charleroi. The concern of proponents of BI is to counter exclusion even more than to end poverty. The condition of being unemployed, not permitted to work because one is receiving benefit, is a condition of exclusion from the ordinary interests of the greater part of society. During two sessions I found an opportunity to inject this argument. People sitting near me asked about it with interest, but no comment came from the speakers who were being questioned. I realised that whatever the interpreters were saying in the other languages coming from the various interpreters booths, they were not relaying my questions. When 1 next put up my hand I said there seemed to be some misunderstanding and referred to Allocation Universelle. This helped a little.

Readers may feel that I am straying from language to economics. Well, I needed concrete examples of inefficiency. I proposed to speak about my own experiences, and this, with ecology in general and various aspects of Esperanto, are the topics on which I most often speak. (Oddly enough, there no longer seems to be any need to argue about contraception). Esperanto and BI have much in common; both are designed to help the worst-off, both offer very great advantages to society.

I have not yet referred to another experience which I think most people who attend international meetings can verify from their own experience. When people move out from the various lectures there is a natural tendency to congregate in smaller groups – which speak the same language. To my mind it is important to emphasise that in the context of Esperanto gatherings of any kind this does not happen. Anyone may get into conversation with anyone.

So, two more brief anecdotes. I was recently invited to explain Basic Income to a group of about twenty five young Green Esperanto speakers from eleven countries, including Poland and Albania, who were meeting in Co. Kerry, in the south of Ireland. They were enthusiastic about the proposal; one said it had changed his whole view of the world.

At a Green Co-ordination meeting in Budapest there were more than twenty nationalities taking part over two days with full-time English and French interpreters. Towards the end someone invited the Bulgarian delegate to speak, He came to the podium, explained in a few words that he did not speak English or French. His two days must have seemed long. I addressed him in Esperanto and he replied that he and many of his colleagues spoke the language. This had some benefit. Per Gharton from Sweden, who speaks perfect English and used to chair Green meetings, is now a member of the European Parliament and has spoken strongly in favour of Esperanto.

Before I conclude, I wish to add that I have limited myself carefully to what I have heard with my own ears – or not heard. I have said scarcely anything about my enjoyment of Esperanto. I have not quoted someone far better qualified, Professor Claude Piron, of the University of Geneva, where he teaches psychology, not linguistics. He used to be a translator for the United Nations and the World Health Organisation, competent to oversee translation in five languages. He resigned because of his perception of the wastefulness and inadequacy of the system and returned to the study of psychology. He writes most enjoyably in Esperanto. On this present topic he has written a superbly readable book in French, *Le Dén des Langues*.

I find I can end this paper by a reflection on a conversation with one of my sons, who called to visit us on his way back from Helsinki recently. He spends his life observing and drawing birds and had been invited to give a talk to Finnish ornithologists. Of course he had enjoyed himself; the Irish Ambassador had invited him to dinner, with his Finnish friends. But how had the talk gone? 'All right, but of course it was translated, so I had to stop and wait after every couple of sentences'. I replied that this was a good example of the need for Esperanto. He answered that if he had spoken in Esperanto they would not have understood him. He took it for granted that they would not. He did not know that the Finnish Ministry for Education had made enquiries and reported that it would be desirable to teach the international language in all primary schools.

But the damage was had already been done, shortly after my first birthday, in September 1922.

The League of Nations, having heard a report from twenty four experts on the need for a 'help-language' declared in favour of a neutral and simplified language and chose Esperanto. It was agreed that all member states should introduce this in primary schools and report back. But alas! the French Minister for National Instruction ordered his influential delegates to 'drown the push for Esperanto'. They managed to have this decision postponed. The Japanese Deputy Secretary General, Nitobe, said that in twenty years' time, that is in 1942, the League would be ridiculed for this delay.

It has been a long delay. If it had not happened, if the words of the Emperor of Japan had been understood, the Atom bomb might not have been dropped on Hiroshima. Who can tell? Would the war have happened? Would we be discussing the languages of the European community?

Keep the best till last.

In an article about language learning published in *The Irish Times* in January 1971 a paragraph opens with, 'My motivation towards learning Greek has a long history of latency'. I explain that, aged ten, I was asked by visiting relatives whether I liked school. I replied that it was well enough, but I would prefer to learn Latin and Greek, 'like Tom Brown's Schooldays'. Five years later, reading Boswell, I learnt that Dr. Johnson's protégée, Mrs. Williams, had taken up the study of Greek at the age of 70, so I decided that there was no hurry. Another five years passed and in the library of the (then) Colegio de los Nobles Irlandeses in Salamanca, the Rector assured me that I could easily learn to read Homer.

I regret that I have not done so, but when I wrote that 1971 article I was engaged in studying New Testament Greek in extra-mural classes in UCD while also having a renewed encounter with German in the Goethe Institut. I was then aged 49, so before I compare those experiences I had better go further back.

If I regret Homer I much more regret that, while I was coming up to age seven, living for a while in Kenmare, my parents sent me to the Convent National School. Here at some time in the day we stood in a semi-circle and read from a faded, very simple, English primer. At other times we sat in desks and looked at small books with different letters in them. The other children would say something. I don't believe that I would, though I might copy what I heard; I noted that when the number 7 appeared people said 'agus'.

This might have given me some insight into the experience of children who are baffled by reading, but my situation was different. I could read English with ease; Mother Superior had examined me, had given me a page of her Missal to read. No one suggested that inability to read Irish was a shortcoming. I did not even know that which I was not reading was a *language*, much less my theoretical mother-tongue. They could have explained; about that time I remember my mother showing me a small book with benediction hymns, *Tantum ergo sacramentum* ... Latin in one column, English in the other, and explaining that the different words had the same meaning. If only my parents had let me stay at home and had asked Maggie, from Castletownbere, to talk with me in Irish. I would have been set up for life. Instead, aged about eight, I found myself in Gibraltar, with two or three Spanish maids instead of one Irish girl and from them I absorbed the fundamentals. The first lesson I remember was given by two workmen re-building the steps outside our house, who taught me how to count, using cigarette cards, *uno, dos, tres, cuatro, cinco, seis*. My father was a thorough hispanophile and laid down a rule that during school holidays I must spend an hour with Hugo's *Spanish in Three Months Without a Master*, correcting my own exercises. [I enjoyed this hour more than than the other hours picking stones out of the garden].

Hugo having been dealt with, my father told me I could buy any books in Spanish that I wished and put them down to his account in the solitary bookshop. Sexton Blake was satisfactory, then historical romances by Rafael Sabatini which I supposed him to have written in Spanish. At that time we could and did drive freely into Spain; Gibraltar's local paper in Spanish, *El Calpense,* was delivered as well as the English-language one and there were always Spanish journals, such as ABC in the house.

I should think I was eleven or twelve by the time my father gave me the handsomely bound Spanish Missal. This had not only what is called the ordinary of the Mass but the texts of the Proper for all the Sundays of the year in parallel columns of Latin and Spanish. This was no novelty; the amiable Mother Superior of the convent in Kerry had bestowed a full daily Missal on my mother with a Sunday Missal for me on our departure. My parents and I went to Mass every morning. The celebrant always spoke Latin as his predecessors had been doing for well over a thousand years, until the tectonic shift in the early 1970s. When reading the Spanish Missal, hearing the Latin text spoken, I did not notice my eyes drifting over to the Latin side, so that I later found it easy to understand the Vulgate -St. Jerome's translation of the Bible. I also grew to love the interspersed poetry.

Whenever our parish priest said a Mass for the Dead a colleague of his would play the organ and sing the *Dies Irae,* so that became familiar; it was amazing to hear the same music, same words sung perfectly by a Chinese choir in Beijing in 1986, when Latin had melted away in Ireland. Later I may explain why I was in Beijing.

To return to acquaintance with Spanish; we left Gibraltar in 1939; I was able to live for year in Spain, first in Segovia, then in Salamanca where I enrolled in a course for foreigners in the University and also attended the lectures that interested me. The fortunes of war cut short this stay.

As for French, I had been taught this in the ordinary way in school, but never by a native speaker. Perhaps because in reading Spanish I went through available classics, starting with the Canción del Cid, on to Cervantes, Lope de Vega, Calderon, Fray Luis de Leon, I took a similar path in French starting with the Roman de Roland enjoying Villon, Ronsard, right through the complete works of Molière [Gibraltar's Garrison Library had been well stocked] up to Mauriac being unhappy among the pines. I do not know whether anyone will recognise the names of Hilaire Belloc and D B Wyndham Lewis whom I used to read and who assumed that if one was literate, one understood French.

This may be the place to observe that 'understanding' was then quite widely accepted as the normal goal of language learning. It in this light that T S Eliot recommended that the way to enjoy Dante was to read the *Divina Commedia* in the three small bilingual volumes of the Temple Classics. I took this advice and did profit by it. In fact, I spent my first month's pay as a student nurse on those little books; £1 bought the set. What's more, I read the last cantos of *Paradiso* while sitting in the sun on a grassy bank on St. Patrick's Purgatory, Lough Derg, waiting for the boat to bring me back to ordinary life.

Irish was a different matter, I had been back to Ireland for about a year and had been taught some Irish in two different schools (both Loreto like Gibraltar, so familiar enough). In one school I was in first year, in the next I was placed in third year. I liked and memorised some poems, but did not get a grip on the language, though I wanted to. When I returned after that year in Spain, aged nineteen, I found a very good Gaelic League class for beginners. If I had been able to continue I might have made progress, but I was called up for nursing and that was the end of that, because after nursing there was physiotherapy and after that marriage and a family.

And so I reached age 49, having been a freelance journalist for several years. Our five younger children were at St Kilians Deutscheschule; I had some free mornings and decided to join a beginners' class in the Goethe Institut. Not a complete beginner; while snowed up in Segovia I had bought two years of a school German course, in Spanish; I memorised all the strong verbs. The course in New Testament Greek was offered to people who had been attending

Extra Mural lectures in Bible study given by Professor Dermot Ryan who shortly afterwards became Archbishop of Dublin. I saw material for an article in contrasting the grammar-based Greek lessons with the deft refusal of our German teacher to mention that in the accusative the masculine article changes while the feminine and neuter article remain unchanged. I also commented on the introduction of oral examinations for the Leaving Certificate.

Fast forward from 1971 to 1979. I had in the meantime done a three-week intensive course in German, *Deutsch Aktiv*, an excellent course, very well taught but I would have needed an extended stay in Germany to become fluent. Years, I think. But a visit to Vienna in 1979 opened a magic door. I was with my husband; we had taken advantage of an economy return flight but we had no money to spare. My husband noted that entry to the Esperanto-Museo in the Hofburg was free; he had been introduced to the language when he was a boy scout. We went. We found large, bright rooms full of books and papers. We were given some newsletters. I did not look at these until long after we were home again, but when I did I found there was a good deal that I could understand: that the Museo had been founded in 1927 by Felix Zamenhof, brother of Dr. Lazaro Ludoviko Zamenhof; that it had been closed by the Nazis in 1938, that there were medical and other congresses taking place in different parts of the world, all speaking Esperanto.

No need to detail the enquiries that at last put me in touch with Christopher Fettes, in St. Columba's College, almost a neighbour. He explained that the five letters with 'supersignoj' ĉ ĝ ĵ ĥ and ŝ permit unvarying grapheme/phoneme correspondence and that the stress is always on the penultimate syllable. This means that one can feel safe reading aloud within a few hours of acquaintance. It certainly saves time if one can have some instruction, but the language was designed by a very remarkable young man, designed specifically for self-instruction, in the hope that it could be learnt by people from any linguistic background. Since it is used for yearly meetings by young Japanese, Chinese and Koreans, since I receive tourism invitations from Samarkand and Uzbekisthan and Tallin and have taken up an offer to visit Andhra Pradesh it appears that he designed it well. So well, in fact, that Hitler singled out his family for extermination.

But our topic is Lifelong Language Learning, not the history of any one language. My experience has been that I learnt to understand and find considerable enjoyment in several Indo-european languages and by the good fortune of youth found myself able to speak and write one, but only one, fairly confidently; since that was luck, not learning, it is of doubtful relevance. The contrast with Esperanto is striking. I was almost sixty when I met it. I learnt it largely from general reading, specifically from *La Tuta Esperanto* by Henrik Seppik. When I met a multinational collection of

Esperanto speakers, I found I could discuss anything with anyone.

It combines simplicity with flexibility. Since nouns are not burdened with gender and all verbs are regular, one feels relatively free from fear of mistakes. Every root can be given any role, as noun, adjective, verb, adverb, indicated by the ending. This does not mean that one is excused from thinking about what one is saying; the advantage is that one can say what one is thinking, without trawling for apposite idiom chunks. The historic retention of an accusative case, scorned by experts, was almost certainly a recipe for survival.

As I have said, I met Esperanto in 1979, began to investigate it a year later. In 1983 I found myself free, for the first time in many, many years, to be regularly absent from home and study for a graduate diploma in linguistics. My interest was to find out whether Esperanto was as exceptional as it seemed to me. Every comparison I met indicated that it is indeed exceptional, with potential usefulness running to waste.

Just one example: in Bernard Comrie's *Universals and Linguistic Typology* there is a discussion of relativization, giving examples from a great variety of languages, showing the different extent to which they can relativize and how these differences make up pattern. Malagasay, for example, can relativize only the subject. One can say 'The student saw the woman'. The student being the subject, it is possible to say, 'The student who saw the woman', but not 'The woman whom the student saw'. In English it is possible to relativize the subject, the direct object, the non-direct object and the possessor, when there is one. Other languages have varied possibilities. How does the inquisitive linguist investigate the impossibilities? It seems that a shared knowledge of Esperanto, which, of course, has as many options as English, and which is increasingly being acquired by speakers of lesser-used languages, including Malagasy, could have a helpful role.

More immediately, I would like to observe that there is here a language which was designed to help word peace, which would not only save the UN and the EU and other such bodies vast sums of money and help them to be more efficient but which is also peculiarly well suited as a second language for adult literacy and as one response to the Mature Learner's Dilemma.

Dyslexia, in the sense of difficulty in learning to read, is practically unknown in Italy. In Italian there is a fairly close match between phonemes (sounds) and graphemes (written letters or letter groups). French children have more problems: about 36 phonemes, represented by 190 graphemes.

English uses 62 phonemes represented by *1,120* graphemes. Dyslexia is a plague in English-speaking countries. Further, English researchers selected the 500 most frequently used words in English and found that, between them, they shared about *14,000* different meanings.

This may be why native speakers of English are in demand.

In Esperanto every word is spoken as it is spelled, and vice versa. Each word has one meaning, but because words may be easily composed and clearly understood, it has peculiar advantages for international use – as a *second* language, to protect every first language from erosion.

I am Irish; the Irish language has almost disappeared, drowned in English.

Some observations on the role of the Case System in Esperanto

1 Love at first sight

There is a risk in using the word 'Esperanto' in the title of a paper. Claude Piron recounts meeting during some reception a French linguist who asked him, 'Was he by any chance the author of *Le Défi des Langues?'*

'A remarkable book; most informative and agreeably written. I congratulate you. Of course, when I came to the word "Esperanto", I read no further'.

Piron had taken care to describe actual linguistic confusion and common illusions about language learning in the first two-thirds of the book before even mentioning a possible remedy.

Others react in a different way. When they chance to come across a language which they can use as their own, without looking over their shoulders to remember what 'native speakers' might say, and which does not require any accent except clarity, they feel positive curiosity. Of these I was one. When I had read a few books and attended a conference of people from about thirty countries, with all of whom I could discuss any subject that presented itself (everyone helped and I had a dictionary) I was offered the opportunity to study for a graduate diploma in theoretical linguistics. This seemed to be an excellent opportunity to evaluate my new language.

2 Investigation

The course was in every way a valuable and enjoyable educational experience. This is not the place to enlarge on the benefits of language awareness. My focus now is on my observation that Esperanto is not only useful, but is also interesting from the point of view of linguistics. English-speaking linguists are inclined to brush it to one side. In this paper I suggest that Fillmore's *The Case for Case* (1968) provides a framework for investigation. When I read his paper I recognised an enquiry that harmonised with my own initial interest in Esperanto and recognised how important the question of case marking is in that language. It was only after further enquiry that I realised that the so-called accusative case was central to its development and probably to its survival. It seemed also that during the evolution of Esperanto the case sysem mutated slightly in a way that may support the views of Fillmore in *The Case for Case Reopened.*

3 History and comparisons

Because Esperanto is a planned or 'artificial' language, and because this accusative case was so much debated during its early years, more than a century ago, it is necessary to outline the history, not only of Esperanto, but of the principal planned languages which were put into circulation at about the same time, or later. Indeed, the existence of these various language projects, at roughly the same time and place, provides opportunity for observations not so very different from research projects set up compare plant growth or child development. Well known linguists Jespersen and André Martinet, were involved in some of the parallel projects. In a sociological survey The *Esperanto Movement* (Foster 1982) the author says that it is not surprising that little is known in the outside world about the Esperanto movement since so much of the documentation is in Esperanto. (The most complete documentation of the early development is published in Japan.) Foster believed that:

> the Esperanto movement provides interesting material for students of comparative linguistics, international politics, peace and conflict research and contemporary European history.

It is important to understand the origin of Esperanto, to know that it was not designed by a theorist but by a boy who knew nothing of the long history of attempts to find a 'universal language'. He says himself:

> The idea to which I have dedicated my whole life appeared to me – ridiculous as it may seem to say so – in my earliest infancy, and from that time has never left me.
>
> (Letter to Nikolaj Borokovo, cited in *Esperanto, the New Latin for the Churches,* Matthias, 2002)

He was born in Bialystok, at that time in Russia, among Russians, Poles, Germans and Jews and became convinced that multiplicity of languages was the chief cause that divided human beings and made them into unfriendly units. The child Ludwik decided that when he grew up he would design a language that would be simple enough for everyone to learn. By his fifth or sixth year in the Gymnasium (Classical Academy) he had designed his first version and shared it with his classmates. He designed his language independently, using as resources his knowledge of Russian, Polish, Hebrew, German, Latin, Greek and French. In the context of this paper it is important to understand that the 'accusative case' was *not* built into it because he was accustomed to case languages. He indicated that when he encountered English he was impressed by its relative simplicity. But he continued to work on his language until he found that he could say:

> I can assert with certainy that it is no longer an insubstantial shadow of whatever language I might be occupying myself with at the time; it has gained its own individual aura, its own soul, its own life, its own characteristic physiognomy, its own expressions independent of any influence. The language flowed of its own accord, flexible, elegant and completely free, just like the living mother tongue.

His method of occupying himself with an established language included pruning away features that seemed inessential. As will appear later, one feature that he positively did not prune away was an accusative case.

4 Questioning Chomsky

Noam Chomsky now fights other battles, but when I studied linguistics his name carried great weight. *Language and Responsibility* (1979) contains a report of a conversation with Mitsou Ronat:

> MR 'Then you can compare the failure of artificial languages with the failure of utopian societies?'
>
> NC 'Perhaps. One cannot learn an artificial language constructed to violate universal grammar as readily as one learns a natural language, simply by being immersed in it. At most, one might conceive such a language as a game, a puzzle ...

Now, if there exists a planned, 'artificial' language, which one *can* learn by being immersed in it, or alternatively learn by instruction or self-instruction in the same way in which one might learn any ethnic language, and if it is usual to find that, in proportion to the time and effort invested, one has acquired very much greater command and confidence in this language than in ethnic languages which one has studied, is it not reasonable to claim that this language *does not* violate universal grammar?

And, if it does not violate universal grammar, does that not mean that it must be congruous with universal grammar (always supposing that the concept of universal grammar is valid)? The implication must be that such a language can properly form part of research into Universal Grammar.

The conversation quoted above was, by the way, conducted in two languages, Chomsky speaking English, Ronat speaking French, a convenient solution in some circumstances. I am reminded of the Great Lexicographer:

> While Johnson was in France he was generally very resolute in speaking Latin. It was a maxim with him that a man should not let himself down, by speaking a language which he speaks imperfectly. Indeed, we must often have observed. how inferior, how like a child a man appears who speaks a broken tongue.
>
> Boswell, Life of Dr. Samuel Johnson, ref. to 1775

Chomsky mentioned learning by immersion. 'Immersion' may mean that children learn it when it is the language of the home – many couples who have different mother-tongues use Esperanto at home; others do so because they have met each other through Esperanto. The children are referred to as *'denaski esperantistoj'* and naturally take it for granted. There is also a system of teaching by carefully planned direct method, the 'Cseh metodo' which is notably popular in Eastern Europe, in Africa and, I understand, in Brazil. This works well and is appropriate to classes with mixed linguistic background and to people who may not be literate, but I feel a need to acknowledge a personal prejudice: I find the grammar so economical and elegant that I suspect that students who bypass grammar miss a work of art.

It is not surprising that a language which has Latin, Greek and Slavonic roots and is completely regular should be readily learnt in Europe. The welcome given to it by both Chinese and Japanese is more surprising. The Chinese monthly *El Popola Ĉinio* reported that it was being studied by a variety of people in every province of China, while a speaker at the 64th World Congress of Esperanto said:

> The European languages are difficult enough for Chinese and also for other Orientals. That is, for a quarter, a half or possibly even more of the human race; at the same time, Chinese is even more difficult for westerners. The international language needs therefore to be the easiest for both. Come to that, Esperanto is not so easy for us, but it is very much easier than any national language.

This appeal was backed up by an announcement from the Chinese Ministry of Education during a congress in 1983 that Esperanto was to be considered equal to any other foreign language in schools and universities, for examinations, research and promotion.

Acceptance on each side of the globe, whether they are called 'East' or 'West' favours the proposal that Esperanto is congruent with

Universal Grammar. Comrie (1981) says there are two radically different views of language universals and of language universal research; one of which, Chomsky's, advocates detailed study of an individual language and holds that language universals are innate properties of the human, while the other, advocated by Greenberg, requires research into a large range of languages as data base and has an open mind on possible explanations for lamguage universals

I venture to suggest that observation of the varying fates of a set of planned or artificial languages may have something to contribute to such research.

4 The Case for Case

Charles Fillmore's *The Case for Case* (1968) and *The Case for* Case *Reopened* (1977) relate to a category which is of great significence in the structure of Esperanto and perhaps equally significant in its absence from the other contemporary planned languages.

The Case for Case opens with the words, 'speculation on language universals has not always and everywhere been viewed as a fully respectable pastime for a scientific linguist'. The author adds that times have changed; that this essay is intended as contribution to the study of formal and substantive syntactic universals, and that it will plead that the grammatical notion of 'case' deserves a place in the base component of the grammar of every language. He says that studies which look simply at the semantic functions of inflectional affixes miss valid insights, and that in them 'a conception of base structure in which such concepts as "subject" and direct "object" are missing'. The latter are regarded as belonging only to the surface structure of some (but possibly not all) languages.

Fillmore adds that two assumptions are essential to the development of the argument: the centrality of syntax and the importance of covert categories. He asserts that we are constantly finding that grammatical features found in one language show up in some form or other in different languages as well, if we have the subtlety to discover covert categories.

Some other passages from this paper will be seen to relate to the structure and development of Esperanto. Firstly, the discussion of prepositions in English, which Fillmore says are selected on the basis of several types of structural features, in ways exactly analogous to those which determine particular case features in Latin: identity of surface subject or object, occurrence after particular verbs, etc. He says that the only difficulty in recognising the analogy lies in the fact that even the most elaborate case languages may have combinations of prepositions with case forms.

On p. 19 ff. he mentions some views of Greenberg, Lehmann and Jespersen which are particularly interesting in the present context. Greenberg has remarked that cases cannot be compared across languages – two case systems may have different numbers of cases, the names of the cases may conceal functional differences, but case *uses* may be expected to be comparable. Fillmore, not surprisingly, disagrees with Greenberg's recommendation that cross-linguistic study of case-uses should be presented only in connection with true case languages. He also disagrees with Cassidy ('case' will be properly used and will continue to have some meaning only if the the association with inflection be fully recognised) and Lehmann (To us a particular case is non-exisent unless it is represented by forms which contrast in a system with others).

Fillmore's own view is that if intrasentence relationships (of the type discussed in case-systems) can be shown to be comparable across languages, and if there is some predictive or explanatory use to which assumptions concerning the universality of these relations can be put, then surely there can be no meaningful objection to using the word 'case' in a clearly understood deep structure sense, to identify these relationships.

It is just this phrase '... some predictive or explanatory use to which assumptions concerning the universality of these relations can be put' which suggests that Fillmore would understand the determination of the initiator of Esperanto to keep the accusative affix in sight – as if he were building a lighthoue on submerged rocks. Natives may take it for granted that the rocks are there, but if you are expecting mariners from all over the world markers are required.

Fillmore refers to Jespersen. To Jespersen it is wrong to speak of 'analytic' cases, even when there is no 'local' meaning in the preposition phrases, because 'cases' are one thing and 'preposition-plus-object-constructions' another. Jespersen's position is coloured a little by his belief that the caselessness of English represents a state of progress for which we ought to be grateful. Fillmore adds in a footnote a quotation from Jespersen, giving his own italics to these words:

> *If the English language has gone farther than the others in simplifying thes rules, then we should be devoutly grateful and not go out of our way to force it back into the disorder and complexity of centuries ago.*

It is all the more interesting in this context we find that Jespersen had been closely associated with one of the contemporary 'planned languages' and had designed another, both, as we shall see, taking negative attitude to case structure

5 Contemporary planned languages

As Pei (1969) writes, since the days of Descartes, Wilkins and Comenius, at least a thousand proposals of one description or another for an international language have been advanced. More recently Umberto Eco in *La Ricerca della lingua perfetta nella cultura europea* (1993) explores in detail these and some of their elaborate predecessors and praises Esperanto's retention of the accusative. Based on a series of lectures in the

Collège de France in 1992-93, it has been translated into many languages, into English as *The Search for the Perfect Language*,

In the introduction he says that so much and so various is the material at his disposal, he decided to concentrate on the *history of the idea.* 'This work seeks only to follow, according to their main features and using examples, the history of Utopia during almost two thousand years'. If one compares the English translation with that in Esperanto, it appears that the latter is the better adapted to Eco's intricate investigations. Only a handful, comparatively close in time and in design, require to be mentioned here. When I attended my first Universala Kongreso de Esperanto I bought *Planlingvaj Problemoj* by William Gilbert (1962). Gilbert had been an advocate of Occidental from 1932 until 1948. Then he began to have doubts and studied Interlingua. By 1950 he had made up his mind that, however agreeable the naturalist languages might appear to Westerners, Esperanto was the only one that had had the possibility of becoming a world language. From this thorough knowledge he was able to give interesting detailed comparisons of three planned languages. At this point the competing languages should be listed, with survival rates, if available.

1879 Volapük Intricate scheme of declensions and conjugations; considerable vogue for a time; taught in schools; several congresses/ survived until 1911

1885 Passilingua author, Steiner. Survival rate non known.

1887 Esperanto Ludvik Zamenhof was the instigator. Globally active; has found its ecological niche on the Internet.

1889 Mondolingvo. Shortlived.

1903 Latine since flexione No system of derivations; scant grammar.

1907 Ido Result of schism in esperanto; survived until 1943

1922 Occidental result of schism in Ido. Still exists

1927 Novial Designed by Jespersen; did not survive his death in 1943

1950 Interlingua financed by I.A.L.A. Andre Martinet involved, but dissatisfied.

Until researching this paper, though I had known of the existence of these various projects I had had no idea of the emotional struggles that had been sustained between the opponents of the accusative case, the prophets of naturalism and the lone young doctor from Warsaw who had done so much writing and translating in his lingvo internacia that he knew what worked and what did not. He summarised this the skeleton of this language in sixteen rules. The first two rules are:

Parts of speech

1. there is not indefinite article; there is only one definite article, **la**, which is invariable.

2. Nouns (substantives) are formed by adding **o** to the root. To form the plural **j** is added. (English speakers may be reminded of Greek plural: *hoi polloi).* There are two cases, nominative and accusative; the accusative is formed by adding **n** to the nominative. Equivalents of other cases are formed by the use of prepositions (e.g **de mia patro**, my father's)

Both Ido and Novial (the two with which Jespersen was concerned) have a non-compulsory accusative. Commenting on this, Gilbert writes:

> The speaker who is not in the habit of using an accusative may forget it precisely when it is needed to avoid misunderstanding. The listener, for his part, cannot tell whether the absence of an accusative is intentional or not. As Professor Bjorn Collinder remarks in *La Problemo de la Lingvo Internacia,* these reformers provide an accusative ending in the well known style of the railway alarm system, *Only to be used in case of genuine danger.* The non-compulsory accusative, just like the alarm brake, is most often useless, because one is aware of the danger only after the catastrophe ...We must admit that many esperantists quite often forget the accusative or use it incorrectly; it requires certain syntactic analysis, usually quite simple, but occasionally more complex. We do not hide from ourselves the disadvantages of an obligatory accusative, but it gives the phrase in Esperanto a precision

> and flexibility, the advantages of which are almost immeasurable. Correct use of the accusative makes misunderstanding almost impossible. In the competing language projects correct language use does not give any guarantee against misunderstanding. It is here the difference lies, and it is crucial for an international language.

[Gilbert gives as example in Occ *Occidental, quel clar subtene li heredat classic cultural base de Europa, es li natural lingue commun del cultivat Occidente.* This could mean that Occidental either upholds, or is upheld by, the cultural base of Europe. It also implies that it does not even aim to non-European peoples].

6 Linguists eager to improve La Internacia(n) Lingvo(n)

Young Zamenhof had produced a workable language while he was still at school; his classmates celebrated its birthday with a party; this was in 1878. It was in this year that Volapük was published. Zamenhof investigated it and objected to its many arbitrary features. However, it flourished for some years, while he was compelled to put his language to one side when a medical student in Moscow. When he returned home he found that his father had destroyed his notes, so he had to make a fresh start; by 1885 he was satisfied that the language had a life of its own and he explained it in four booklets, in Russian, Polish,

German and French, but could not find a publisher.

In 1887 he married Klara Zilbernik and she gave him all the money at her disposal to enable him to publish the brochures himself, using the name 'Dr. Esperanto' in order that his medical practice should not suffer. He sent them, in appropriate languages, to newspaper editors and well-known persons and institutions. Replies and questions, some written in the new language, resulted. All four brochures are reproduced in the *Fundamento de Esperanto.*

The correspondence brought at once support and problems. Support from Christian Schmit in Nuremberg who in 1889 published a journal *La esperantisto* of which Zamenhof became editor. He was very poor; an offer from another German, Trompeter to fund the journal and also pay a small sum to its editor was very welcome. But Trompeter was anxious for a few changes, as were other critics. Answering these critics consumed more time and energy than Zamenhof, who had to make a living as a doctor, could spare.Forster writes that:

> it is reasonable to consider the kind of changes that the various reformers might propose. There was a certain amount of agreement about the weak points of Esperanto, though not usually agreement about what could be put in their place. The alphabet was one target for criticism. Zamenhof had adopted the principle, 'one symbol, one sound'. For this purpose he had to introduce some extra consonants, ĉ, ĝ, ĥ, ĵ, ŝ. Another objection was commonly made to

> the existence of an accusative case, formed by the addition of the letter -n; *hundo,* dog, becomes *hundon* in the accusative. The opponents of this pointed out that the accusative mark was absent in English and French and that Esperanto should be more simple than natural languages, not more difficult. A further objection was to the concord of adjectives and nouns in the plural.

It is not easy to understand why people who seemed to appreciate the language should wish to rid it of such crucial elements, but Trompeter was so eager for these changes that in 1884 he said he would withdraw his support if the reforms were not introduced. Zamenhof's generosity had placed him in peculiar difficulty. In the *Unua libro* he had written, in each language:

> An international language, like a national one, is the property of society and the author renounces all personal rights in it forever

Unlike the inventor of Volapük, he handed over his language to those who would use it. Now influential users wanted to remove its backbone. He had long ago experimented with the proposed changes. He knew that now the language 'flowed of its own accord, flexible, elegant and completely free'. There had been time to observe the fact that the original scheme worked in practice. He saw this as far more important than theoretical proposals, but to be consistent with his own statement he had to have the consent of enough users. A ballot was the only way. He reluctantly began to suggest areas for possible changes, including those already mentioned and the replacement of many teutonic and slavonic roots. This scheme was presented as a package to be voted on by the subscribers to *La esperantisto.*

I cannot avoid a suspicion that the replacement of teutonic and slavonic roots was a prudent inclusion by Zamenhof himself, because before the actual vote he wrote privately to St. Petersburg Esperanto Society, which he knew to be conservative in matters of language and *urged members to become individual subscribers so that they would be entitled to vote.*

In two ballots the subscribers voted to retain the language unchanged. Trompeter than withdrew his financial support, though he continued as an individual subscriber until his death in 1901. Zamenhof was poor enough already; his father-in-law had to help feed the family, but Ludovik took sole charge of the journal until it was suppressed by the Tsarist authorities in 1895. Their motive was the publication of a translation of an article by Leo Tolstoy, 'Prudence or belief'.

The *esperantistaro,* the dispersed adherents of the young language could not survive or develop without a means of intercommunication. A new journal was published for a short time in Bulgaria; in 1895, with money from Russian and Swedish supporters, *Lingua internacia* was published in Uppsala. Living up to its name, it moved for some years to Budapest, then, in 1902, to Paris. Here an energetic group linked with others in England and organised the first Esperanto Congress in 1905, at Boulogne sur Mer. Six hundred and eighty eight people from forty different countries came together and talked ecstatically to one another. Zamenhof gave an impressive speech. A vital agreement was reached: the only foundation, compulsory for all esperantists, was the Fundamento; 'Esperanto has no particular master and depends on no particular man'.

The proof that the language flowed as easily in speech as in writing, the acceptance of the *Fundamento,* were, naturally great sources of satisfaction for its initiator. He was observed in Boulogne, 'wandering as if in a dream, his whole body trembling, his composure preserved with difficulty'. But his dream was of world peace; he was not allowed to live peacefully with his language. Pressure for 'reform' continued, in spite of the acceptance of the *Fundamento.* In 1906 two reformers went so far as to offer him 250.000 francs if he would accept certain reforms; this would have enabled him to relinquish his medical practice and give all his time to Esperanto. They did not realise that the language to which he could give his time would not continue to be the one he had designed.

There followed the unhappy Ido schism and stressful debates about idealism and practicality. All that concerns this paper is that, apart from apparent willingness to change, while he was quietly arranging to have more voters on his side, Zamenhof was prepared to make any sacrifice to avoid fundamental changes, especially to avoid discarding the accusative case. It was not he who singled out the accusative, but his critics, but it is still significant that he was prepared to meet them half way in respect of other features, like the alphabet, while he seems to have felt that the accusative, with the positive charge of information that it carries, was essential for an international language. The rivals of this language were supported by experts, or by funding, or by both; Esperanto has survived.

7 Developments

The survival of a language which upholds the centrality of syntax and the desirability of case-marking when the 'control' languages have melted away appears to support Fillmore's assumptions. May one say that, though covert categories are sufficient in national languages where speakers have pragmatic support, categories need to stand up and be counted when speakers have no shared background? That deep structures become transparent in Esperanto?

Only the first two of the Sixteen Rules of Esperanto grammar have been quoted. Two others are relevant to this paper:

> Rule 13, to show motion towards, nouns take the accusative case
>
> Rule 14: each preposition has a definite fixed meaning; but if the sense does not indicate which should be used, recourse may be had to the preposition **je**, which has no meaning of its

own. Alternatively, the accusative without a preposition may be used.

The use of accusative marking to signify motion towards: *Muso kuras en la ĉambro, La muso kuras en la ĉambro**n*** There's a mouse running in the room, The mouse is running **into** the room, is not an invention of Zamenhof's; he adopted it from German, or from some of his other languages. **Je** also comes from German, but it is adapted, not adopted. In German it is flexible, but seems to belong to idiom chunks and to even take the place of the most troublesome moneme in Esperanto: Po. German, *sie zahlen je 3 Mark,* they paid three Marks each. Zamenhof brilliantly gave it a new career as an all-purpose preposition, something an English sub-editor would love to have. The final sentence above, 'Alternatively, the accusative without a preposition may be used', has made it acceptable to use it in expressions of time, measure and value, in each case showing the degree to which some quality or action extends:

He stayed three hours	*Li restis tri horojn*
A man twenty years old	*Viro aĝa dudek jarojn*

These examples taken from the *Concise Esperanto and English Dictionary,* Wells, (1969), are, of course, correct, but 'Dudek jaraĝa viro' would seem more natural. Much more common are such phrases as. *Ni renkontiĝos merkredon,* 'We'll meet on Wednesday', or *'La dekkvinan Augusto ĉiam estas festo* 'The fifteenth of august is always a feast day'.

However rule 14 says that if the preposition has no fixed, definite meaning recourse may be had to the preposition **je.** It goes on to say, alternatively the accusative without any preposition may be used. It seems that conflation of these two possibilities, the substitution of *je* for any other preposition, followed by the substitution of **n** for **je** has brought about the possibility of using the affix *-n* instead of any preposition.

Seppik (1937) explains the use of an apparent accusative with an intransitive verb as in *Tiel li vivis sian tutan vivon* as an abbreviation of *Tiel li vivis dum sia tuta vivo.* It could equally well be accounted for as the saying of a native speaker of English, who can easily say, 'He lived hiis whole life in a state of remarkable innocence'.

Seppik, who for many years taught Esperanto in Norway, Sweden and Czechoslovakia by the direct method, was familiar with students' most frequent mistakes. He wrote *La Tuta Esperanto* in order to help other teachers and to make the potential of the language as clear as possible to those learning without a teacher. The fact that the book is written entirely in Esperanto makes it doubly valuable; reading it is language-practice, the content is not complicated by references to the student's mother-tongue.

In the quite short section dealing with the accusative he allows such phrases as, *Li sopiras ŝin,* He sighs for her, but says the prepositional form is usually to be preferred. *(Li sopiras je ŝi). Mi dankas vin,* in place of *Mi dankas al vi* is acceptable. [In ordinary life, *'Dankon!* Is usual, and the reply may be *'Ne dankinde!* Not thankworthy]

Seppik makes clear that *'Li instruos nin'* instead of *'Li instruos al ni'* and *'Li instruas geografion'* instead of *'Li instruas pri geografio'* are normal and acceptable, but a double accusative in one phrase, as in *'Li instruas nin geografion'* would be a serious mistake.

This suggests a brief return to Fillmore. In *The Case for Case Re-opened* he speaks of events, such as commercial events, in which two different individuals are involved and the actions of each of the two are part of our understanding of any lexical items that can be used for describing this kind of event in any of its aspects. It seems that constructions with *je* and *-n* accomodate themselves well to translations of Fillmore's examples.

I bought a dozen roses.	*Mi aĉetis dekdu rozojn.*
I paid Harry five dollars	*Mi pagis al Henriko kvin dolarojn.*

I bought a dozen roses from Harry for five dollars.
Mi aĉetis dekdu rozojn de Henriko je kvin dolaroj

I paid Harry five dollars for a dozen roses.
Mi pagis kvin dolarojn al Henriko je dekdu rozoj.

Kvin dolarojn mi pagis al Henriko je dekdu liaj multekostaj rozoj!

8 Conclusion

When I wrote this paper I had been acquainted with Esperanto for two or three years. I have left it more or less as it was written, just deleting superfluous examples and inserting a few conjectures. It was Fillmore's papers that focused my attention on the accusative case. In the years since then I have read and written a great deal more in that language, but it seems to me that I have not read a great deal about the accusative case; I have written more myself. There has been a long battle about participles, the ita/ata debate. There is always dissension about neologisms. There are even a few people who still want to change the alphabet and who send unbeautiful little yellow notes full of w and y. An eminent writer can provide a summary of esperanto grammar, showing endings of nouns, adjectives, verbs but not mentioning the accusative affix. A Polish linguist explains that the preface to Zamenhof's first textbook tells how he analysed the language into independent and invariable units, which could function equally as grammatical and semantic morphemes and how in this he was 70 years ahead of this time. Excellent; but when he lists non-radical morphemes 'tiel ke O. A, I, IS, AS,J, N, ANT, IT, ' I want to interrupt and say, 'but N is more radical than a mere non-radical morpheme!' (Rokicki, 1987).

But Lazarus Ludovik Zamenhof is vindicated. The sacrifices he made to hold onto the accusative marking are rewarded. The outsiders who knew it was 'old fashioned' are gone. But those who use and love Esperanto don't think about the accusative; it's part of the real world, like rain.

INTERCULTURAL SPACES: AN INTERCULTURAL IDENTITY

Food was the first thing that came to mind when I read the words 'Culture' and 'Identity'. In Brussels recently my IBIS hotel had handed out a city map with a circle of icons representing other IBIS hotels; on the map, a larger circle of icons of MacDonalds; I believe they have infected Moscow and Tokyo. Home in Rathfarnham, a local Pizza delivery offers, among others, Original Irish; bacon, egg and sausage pizza.

Instead I find that Language is the main focus, giving a welcome opportunity to call attention to a cohesion of language and identity from which the Irish public is shielded, though it obtains reasonable publicity in the rest of Europe, as well as in Asia. I have decided to arrange this paper around three passages which I hope will stimulate debate.

The first is taken from the end of Roget's preface to the first edition of his monumental organisation of English words and phrases; Roget's *Thesaurus*. This Preface can be found somwhere in each of the many later editions:

> Lastly, such analysis (such as his Thesaurus) can alone determine the principles on which the strictly *Philosophical Language* might be constructed. The probable result of the construction of such a language would be its

> eventual adoption by every civilized nation, thus realizing that splendid aspiration of philanthropists - the establishment of a Universal language ... Is there at the present day,then, any ground for despair,that at some future stage of that higher civilization to which we trust the world is gradually tending,some new and bolder effort of genius towards the solution of this great problem may be crowned with success, and compass an object of such vast and paramount utility?
>
> *Introduction to original edition of Roget's Thesaurus of English Words and Phrases, 1852*

It is clear that Roget took it for granted that if a language which would enable all peoples to share their thoughts and feelings should come to birth it would be welcomed everywhere. It was born in 1887, conceived and nurtured by young boy living in a climate of intercultural hate in Bialystok, then part of the Russian empire. He knew nothing of the search for a philosophical language; he simply believed that if people could understand one another they might be less anxious to kill one another. In the event, it *was* welcomed and was flourishing in 1921/22 when the General Assembly of the League of Nations unanimously agreed that it should be introduced to the primary schools of member states, not only to enable students to communicate across national boundaries, *but also to improve their mastery of their own languages and ability to learn others.*

My next extract, part summary, part quotation, comes from Umberto Eco's book, published in French, Italian, Spanish, Catalan, German,

Esperanto and English. This last translation is not to be recommended. Umberto Eco, in *La Serĉado de la Perfekta Lingvo,*(1993) based on a series of lectures given in the University of Bologna and the Collège de France, says that the theme of the confusion of languages and the attempts to remedy it either by finding or by inventing a language common to the whole human race runs through all cultures.

> The history of perfect languages is a history of failures. But this does not mean that the history of failures is a failure ... The failures were followed by side effects. So much of our theory and practice, from the taxonomy of the natural sciences to comparative linguistics were born as side effects of the search for the perfect language.

The original title in Italian included the words 'nella historia europea'.

But the first chapter (in my esperanto edition) is Ekde Adamo ĝis la *confusio linguarum.* There follows a treasure hunt through time, well worth following. My reason for quoting it here is that the search led Eco to find an 'apostiora' language which he had not known about and which might not be a failure. He devotes pages 269/279 to an examination of Esperanto and a consideration of its practical possibilities. He sees a new respect for minority languages, notes that even in the US, where WASP English was the language of the melting pot, California is now a bi-lingual state, with New York not far behind:

> *Temas pri proceso nehaltigebla. Se la tendenco por Eŭropa uniĝo marŝas samrapide kiel la tendenco al lingo multobliĝo,la sola ebla solvo estos plene adopti eŭropan vehiklan lingvon.*
>
> The principal obstacle now is that seen by d'Alambert: the egoism of governments, which have never distinguished themselves by striving for that which would benefit human society (Eco, 1993)

That is why the Resolution of the General Assembly of the League was deflected. The then French Minister for Public Instruction ordered the head of then French delegation, the philospher Bergson, who was personally favourable, to 'drown this push for Esperanto'. After all, the world already had a superbly clear and logical language: French. (Symoens, 1992)

The political dimension I reserve for my third quotation, and I include autobiography. In Woolworths, probably around 1930, when I was nine, I bought a tiny Esperanto dictionary. I did not encounter the language again until I was sixty, on an economical holiday in Vienna, when my husband spotted the Esperanto-Biblioteca in the Hofburg, entrance free. Three vast, sunny rooms, lined with bookshelves. Our German was limited, he had forgotten the Esperanto he had learnt as a Boy Scout, but the Director gave us couple of mimeographed pages. Months later I looked at them, found I could understand a good deal, sought information and attended an Ecumenical Congress in the Netherlands. This, with 150 people from 30 countries, with whom I was able to join in discussion of anything under the sun, everyone helpful to a beginner, because each had at some time been a beginner, was so exciting that on the way home (by train, bus, boat, another bus another boat) that I quite lost my voice. While I had lost, for a few days, my voice, I had found a new identity.

Of course we all have a range of identities, but for me *esperantisto, samideano* is very near the top. It is not simply a language; I have spoken Spanish since my Gibraltar childhood, read Spanish literature, studied in Salamanca, but do not feel that this has affected my identity, my self-image (except, perhaps, in the matter of food and wine).

A year or so later, the annual Universala Kongreso was held in Budapest. My breakfast companion one morning happened to ask me how I had met Esperanto. I replied that the Director of the Esperanto-Museo in Vienna had given us some information sheets. He was pleased to tell me that he was himself that director. He said, also, that no one would guess from my accent that I spoke English at home.

Home in Dublin, I used my press card to infiltrate a linguistic conference being held in St. Patrick's. I wanted to know what linguists thought about my new language: not much. But during coffee break I was encouraged to do a graduate diploma in theoretical linguistics in Trinity. My mother had died happily earlier in the year so I had fewer responsibilities at home. My first book, *Anything School Can do, YOU Can do Better* had just been a success. I very much enjoyed the experience of guided study. It also helped me to appreciate the clarity and economy of the structure of Esperanto. So often, confronted with one of Chomsky's dilemmas, I would think, 'But that's not a real problem; it's just a problem in English'. Think; not say.

The beauty of Esperanto does not depend only on its clarity and flexibility, or on the independence it gives to expressing what you think without, on the one hand, looking over your shoulder to devine how a native speaker would say it, or on the other, in English, dodging cliches. It was designed to sound beautiful: young Zamenhof was a poet. But the bonus is friendship. Writing this morning to a Japanese bookshop manager, to whom I had sent two dozen copies of my book *€veryone's Own Language,* I take it for granted that this is not a business letter, it's a personal reply to her own friendly questions. She e-mailed me that her stock had sold out; I think there may have been fresh demand because a group of 25 Esperanto speakers who paid a quick visit to Dublin on their way back to Japan from the Congress in Sweden had invited Dubliners to dinner and we had handed out a few copies. We agree, of course, that the purpose of the book is to let Japanese, or Poles, or Spaniards who are struggling to master English know that there is an accessible alternative.

This growing pressure to learn English and the stress and frustration it causes is something I have been reading about on the internet for years. The keynote speech at the opening of the Esperanto congress in Gotenburg recently was given, mainly in French, by Prof. Charles Durand who told us that during the last ten or fifteen years organizations had sprung up in many European countries to protect their respective languages. His message was that there is natural symbiosis between such organizations and Esperanto. A translation of his speech was, of course, distributed to the audience of about 3,000.

He had managed to read his opening paragraph in the local language. By the end of the week he was able to give a farewell speech in competent Esperanto. Similarly, at the end of the previous year's Congress in Brazil the Observer from Unesco expressed, in Esperanto, his admiration of the gathering and his gratitude for the help he had been given during the week to learn the language.

Determination to protect languages is often directed against bullying by the nation-state; Basques against Madrid and Paris; Catalans against Castellano, but by far the greatest alarm is created by the dominance of English and its claim to be the world language. This is exacerbated by advertisements requiring English mother-tongue. Between them different bodies related to the EU Commission released 500 such advertisements in Brussels. The appropriate Commissioner apologised. Such requirements are especially frustrating to people who have spent much effort over many years to become English speakers. Effort is not always enough; few of us recognise how anarchic English is, though we may suspect that its spelling is challenging.

Thinking of our own history we in Ireland may feel that the tidal spread of English is simply a historical phenomenon. If we read Robert Phillipson's book, *English-Only Europe?* (Routledge, 2003) we should change our minds. Phillipson knows how to set out his findings methodically, with a thorough supply of references. If I could be granted one wish, it would be that everyone in Ireland with responsibility in the field of language would read this book, and make it mainstream. The passages I have chosen to quote are short but with cutting edge:

Phillipson, in a chapter discussing global trends in language policy, states that in 1948 George Kennan, the State Department's senior planner, wrote:

> **We have 50 per cent of the world's wealth, but only 6.3 per cent of its population. In this situation, our real job in the coming period is to devise a pattern of relationships which permit us to maintain this position of disparity. To do so, we have to dispense with all sentimentality ... we should cease thinking about human rights, the raising of living standards and democratisation.**

The World Bank and the International Monetary Fund were invented to implement this strategy. Phillipson demonstrates that English is an integral dimension of this globalizaton project, showing that the process of establishing US global hegemony was supported by the expenditure of large amounts of government and private foundation funds in the period 1950–1970.

Four years ago, before Afghanistan and Iraq, we might have thought these propositions far-fetched.

Many of us now believe that Europe is the key to change. Ten or eleven countries, one the birthplace of Esperanto, others in which it is well established, for example Estonia, are being welcomed into the EU, but the EU establishment seems equally set to abandon its principle of giving all member- states equal language rights,

My book, *Everyone's Own Language,* has been recommended as a useful introduction for lesrning the language well and for teaching others. The parish priest of Tory Island is one example who has used it. Its peculiarity is that it advises against translation from one's native language; read, understand, absorb. This was the advice of the Irish linguist, Richard Geoghegan, who translated *La Unua Libro* into English in 1889, while working in Alaska.

It would not convince the Department of Education. In 1997 that Department was given by the EU £3 million in order that European languages should be taught in primary schools. I promptly wrote to the Inspector in charge, suggesting that so many research projects had demonstrated students who first learn Esperanto then make significantly better progess in learning other languages. [The hypothesis is that the concise and transparent grammatical structure of Esperanto gives them a matrix into which they can unconsciously fit the eccentricities of other languages, including their own; further, success in learning one language is acknowledged to promote confidence].

My reply from the Inspector I can describe as a kick in the teeth. A year or so later an IRAAL conference was given a report on the scheme. None of the hearers was enthusiastic about the likely long-term benefits of teaching children French or German for half-an-hour a week. The parents were reported to be very keen.

Incidentally, over years we have carried on correspondence with Ministers, with the NCCA, with schools using Transition Year, etc, which several times gave reason to hope, but which melted way. Folders in my PC are packed with Letters to the Editor which have withered unpublished. Indeed, a few articles about Esperanto were, perhaps by coincidence, the end of my 16 year career as a freelance journalist.

Why? I am inclined to give the credit to Dr. T. Corcoran, Professor of Education in UCD in the early years of the Free State. He believed that in school, children of three could be taught to think in Irish, '... the English thought-ruts not having been sufficiently deepened to prevent the formation of a perfect new system of Irish though-ruts'. Teachers were encouraged to pretend they did not understand English. The Montessori method had been creeping into National School (reported by J. O'Brien, c.1960) but the Reverend Professor condemned it vehemently and seems to have made generations of students ashamed even to think of it. The notion that children might choose their own work he found repugnant.

It is not I who give myself credit for having broken that spell. The mothers who trained as Montessori directors and who undertook to set up their own training centre for adults rather than school-leavers said that one or two articles of mine in *The Irish Times* had set them on their feet. They regularly invited me to their 'open days'. My suggestion is that Corcoran's attitude encouraged negative reaction to language learning in general, as well as undermining Irish.

To conclude my autobiographical skirmishes, I'll report that the Home Education Network invited me to give a keynote talk at their first convention, some years ago. When my eldest son went to school, aged eight, and encountered the leather, I linked up with a few others to get it banned. It is.

With a doctor from the same group, who thought that very large familes contributed to extremely large classes, and five or six others, I helped set up Irish Family Planning.

When the Green Party, Comhaontas Glas, held its twenty first birthday party last year, I cut the Birthday cake. When I had sought information about Esperanto, I was directed to Christopher

Fettes, in St. Columba's College. He and I both believed in Basic Income and a proper land tax. He invited potential supporters to set up a new party, asked me to chair the meeting. Even though Basic Income has not won out, it at least has its own Green Paper.

In Ireland, Esperanto's time has not yet come.

MY EXPERIENCE:

BASIC INCOME, ZAMENHOF, MONTESSORI, TEILHARD DE CHARDIN

On 31 August 1921 Dr. Nitobe Inazou, Deputy Secretary General of the League of Nations, proposed to the Assembly that the International language, known as Esperanto, should be evaluated. This was agreed.

I cannot claim that this was part of my experience, since I was not born until the following day, 1 September 1921, and I could not read his speech until four years ago, but since my perception of an affinity between the concept of Basic Income and that of Esperanto is part of my theme this date provides a convenient opening. The Report that was brought to the Assembly in the following year was so positive that the Assembly unanimously agreed that the language should be introduced to schools in all member countries.

As for myself, I did attend various schools; when Dr. Samuel Johnson, the Great Lexicographer, was asked how best to educate a girl he replied,'Let her loose in a good library'. I was fortunate to have the older parts of the Garrison Library in Gibraltar at my disposal. Later I hoped to paint and draw but felt I should first do something useful; I qualified as a nurse and a physiotherapist. Experience as a nurse let me see how much absurdity may be included in a respected organization. Morning and evening meals for patients consisted mainly of white bread and butter; each evening a nurse offered a wide range of aperients. Large ovens could have baked wholemeal bread.

1st perception: Montessori

The first perception, or insight, relevant to my theme came from observation of my own children learning. When the first baby was few months old her father brought home a book about Dr.Maria Montessori (born in 1870, she was first woman in modern Italy to gain a medical degree) and her understanding of children – her 'didactic material' enables young children to discriminate length, width, weight, temperature, sound, colour etc. and encourages concentration. We lived far from any school; Montessori claimed that children enjoy work and are eager to learn, if they are given some simple materials and allowed choice, including the choice of going away and doing something different. We tried this out with our eight-month old daughter and found that it produced notable satisfaction and enjoyment both for ourselves and for our eleven children, as recounted in *Anything School Can do, You Can Do Better* published to wide acclaim in 1983 by Arlen House.

Further experience showed that the school system was by no means equally effective. The first shock was when our eldest son went to school at the age of eight and found that 'corporal punishment', beating on the hand with a leather strap or a stick was routine in boys' schools. Our son's class counted and found that one brother used the leather sixty times in one morning. (The best teachers, of course, left the leather aside.) This provoked my first involvement in a campaign, in about 1958. At long last Corporal punishment in schools was made illegal in 1983.

2nd perception: National Dividend/Basic Income

Ivan Illich's *Deschooling Society*, which found many echoes, was not published until 1971; I mention it here because it led me towards his later books, including *The Right to Useful Unemployment* published in 1978, about the same time as an ESRI paper on 'Integrated Approaches to Personal Income Taxes and Transfers' which concluded firmly that a National Dividend would be a much more satisfactory solution that any sort of Tax Credit. My enthusiastic recognition that this was both just and practical I count as the second 'perception'. It appeared to be a contemporary version of Jesus' parable of the Workers in the Vineyard, who were properly paid the wage for a day's work, though they had not been fully employed.

Useful campaign experience

Sometime earlier I had become involved in a different campaign. One of the doctors active in opposing beating had argued that children as young as four were sent to join huge classes in school because their mothers had so many babies that they pushed the older ones out to make space. The Vatican Council was in session when our youngest child was born in 1964, just as questions about the wickedness of contraception were being discussed among the better informed clergy and laity of the Catholic Church. My husband Sean and I were among the better informed; for some time I was an associate member of the Irish Theological Association. With the doctor who had been active in defence of children and a few of his colleagues, with the advice of a helpful Jesuit, we set up a clinic for effective family planning, which was not only banned by the Catholic Church but illegal in Ireland.

We called it a Fertility Guidance Clinic. Those were interesting times. Debate in the media, especially in the correspondence pages of the newspapers, which sometimes had to double their space, continued week after week. At our Clinic I was at first the receptionist, who while taking notes re-assured anxious women. Soon it emerged that, as a well informed Catholic mother of eleven, I was best suited to be sent as a speaker in answer to requests from women's groups around the country. This was indeed my motive for involvement. Once I understood that what authority had insisted was sinful was not so, I felt bound to help others also understand this, instead of being either over-burdened or thinking themselves guilty. I had opportunities to explain matters also on radio and television.

I should say that I do not count recognition of the morality of family planning as one of the 'perceptions' which I hope to defend in this paper; contraception would have arrived in Ireland anyway; my concern, as I have said, was to leave women with easy consciences. In this I succeeded, and after four years I handed my job over to practical people. I mention it here because it was a significant part of my experience, the most useful thing I have ever done, and it showed me that half a dozen concerned people can make things happen. Further, since I was twice Irish delegate to conferences of the European Region of IPPF, International Planned Parenthood, it brought me face to face with the language problems of international conferences.

I had opportunities also to explain in print. An article about that youngest son beginning to 'read for meaning' at the age of fifteen months was accepted; the editor asked for more. I found I had become a freelance journalist. My hope was that mothers and fathers who could plan to have just as many children as they could enjoy would also help them to learn and explore their own ability rather than rush them off to school for mass production. Of course I wrote as well about other matters that interested me, for example, our present concern.

Basic Income

Brendan Dowling, the economist who wrote that paper about National Dividend as the remedy for the Poverty Trap, said that the idea should not be dismissed as wild or fanciful; if the familiar Martian observer were to look at the Social Welfare system in position he would diagnose planning by lunatics. Of all the material I read about alternatives that which most impressed me was 'Automation, Employment and the Distribution of Income', by the late Dr. Keith Roberts. I no longer have the book – fools lend books – but remember his statement: economists explain problems; engineers solve them. He, of course, was an engineer. When I wrote a very short argument for BI in the first Green Party manifesto I noted a double absurdity: there is a vast amount of useful work that fails to be done because it does not directly produce profit; as much or more useless or damaging work is done simply because those doing it need an income; yet once a person is labelled unemployed, he or she receives an inadequate income only on condition they do not do any work.

I had a long struggle with the Features Editor of the *Irish Times* to get space for an article on this topic, which I wanted to introduce by telling second-level students that if they were not given a Citizen's Income when they reached the age of 18 they should get involved in politics and fight for it. A half-page article was finally published. This must have been early in 1984 because it led to an invitation to a meeting in Bedford Square in London to discuss 'Social Dividend: The Way Ahead for Income Maintenance?' The Conference was to be held on the 15 May 1984. By chance I have recently found a list of 48 participants, some of them now pillars of BIEN. It was a significant meeting because for most of the participants, whether members of the National League of the Disabled or of One Parent Families this notion was altogether novel. At the end of a day's discussion, when there was almost complete agreement, Dr. Keith Roberts stood beside a flip chart and asked for suggestions for a name for the system we had been discussing. He wrote half a dozen on the chart, then called for votes. BASIC INCOME was the winner.

Of course I joined the new association.

3rd perception: Teilhard de Chardin

That was all very practical, but in the background was another perception which greatly influenced me, keeping in touch with the lively thinking that was then going on in the Catholic Church. *The Phenomenon of Man* by Pierre Teilhard de Chardin was introduced by Sir Julian Huxley who says:

> In the Phenomenon of Man he has effected a threefold synthesis – of the material and physical world with the world of mind and spirit; of the past wih the future; ahd of variety with unity, the many with the one.

Teilhard was a priest, a biologist and a palaeonthologist, whose vision of evolution looked ahead. He saw evolution as a tremendous contribution. No brief quotation can do his thought justice, but it may indicate how I was able to link it to my experience. He says:

> So long as our perspectives of the psychic nature of zoological evolution were based only on the examination of animal lines and their nervous systems, the direction of that evolution remained perforce as vague for our knowledge as the soul itself of those distant relations of ours ... Earlier, when we were discussing the tree of life, we noticed as a fundamental character that brains grew bigger and more differentiated along each zoological stem ... After the transit to reflection, it will henceforth be sufficient to say:'Following each anthropological line, it is mankind that seeks itself and grows'.

Children: the growing point of humanity

Teilhard was born in 1881; his life overlapping with that of Montessori. It is not to be supposed that he ever heard of her but he did say that there was something in our atmosphere that was changing with the course of history. While he said human thinking was the growing point of evolution, she was pointing out that children were much more competent thinkers that had been acknowledged. Education everywhere had hitherto been concerned with forming children in accord with the prevailaing culture; she offered possibilities of development. I had, then already seen a link between two perceptions, between children thinking and the path of human development. If humans are, as Teilhard held, the growing point of evolution, children should be recognised as the growing point of humanity. If so, society should be organised to give the best possible support to children in families. Now it seemed that, in our society, Basic Income would be the system that would best provide such support

4th perception:
Ludwig Zamenhof, a language for humanity

I have said that the influential paper explaining the merits of a National Dividend, commisioned by the Irish Government, was published in 1979. By chance I visited Vienna during that year. My husband, who had met Esperanto when he was a Boy Scout, brought me to the *Esperanto Museo* in the Hofburg. A few pages we were given put me upon enquiry. Eventually this led to Christopher Fettes, who was teaching in St.Columba's College, just a little further up the slopes of the Dublin Mountains than we were ourselves. He explained the essentials, gave me some Chinese Esperanto magazines to read. I read, I went to a small conference in the Netherlands, found the language so congenial that I studied for a graduate diploma in theoretical linguistics in Trinity College; this helped me to realise how very remarkable Esperanto is.

Green politics, Basic Income

Meanwhile Christopher Fettes and I found that, in addition to Esperanto, we both favoured the National Dividend and Site Value Taxation. He decided to invite friends, vegetarians, opponents of vivisection and others to discuss setting up a political party which would put forward policies, which the established parties never thought of, giving special emphasis to Basic Income. He asked me to chair the meeting so that he would be free to speak. The Ecology Party which later became the Green Party, was founded. The Green Group in the European parliament in May, 2002 adopted a Resolution favouring Esperanto as a protection for endangered languages.

At the end of February 2002 the Irish Taoiseach (Prime Minister) was asked in the Dail by the leader of the Green Party, when would the often promised Green Paper on Basic Income be published? Would there be an opportunity to discuss it in the House before the election took place? The Taoiseach gave a lengthy answer, emphasising the complexity, the difficulty of evaluating a system that does not exist elsewhere, but asserting that it would be published in a matter of weeks. After the election is over, the same Taoiseach, Bertie Ahern, has been returned, but there is no sign of the Green Paper. The Green Party also have four new TDs in addition to the two who were members of the previous Dail. I trust they will persist with this question.

Links

So, my experience permits me to discern synergy between Montessori's obervation of children, Teilhard's understanding of evolution and Basic Income. How am I going to find a link with Esperanto, which from my opening paragraph has manifestly been my intention? The first link is very clear to me; I have often repeated it. BI is concerned with justice in respect of distribution of income. This concern must focus on the worst off, those deprived both of discretionary income and of freedom, consequently left behind the rest of their fellow citizens in health, happiness and education. The paradox is that it would countribute to improvements in everyone's health, happiness and education. Esperanto is similar.

Ludovik Zamenhof was born in Bialystok, which was then in Russia, now in Poland, in 1859. Four sets of people lived in the town, Russians, Poles, Germans and Hebrews, each speaking their own language, each an enemy to all the others, too often a murderous enemy. He wrote later that as a child he believed that the unhappy state of language confusion was the principal cause of division and enmity within the human family. At that time it seemed to him that grown-ups could do anything they wished and he resolved that when he grew up he would certainly do away with this evil. By the time he was nineteen he had laid the groundwork for an easily learnt language which would enable people of any background to communicate with each other. His work was interrupted by medical studies in Moscow – while he was away his father burnt all his papers – but in 1887, when he was 26, he published the result in four small brochures in different languages. The money for publication came from his wife's dowry, with her agreement. Among all the thousand or so schemes for a Universal Language, this one was peculiarly benevolent and unselfish; having planned the essential framework, Zamenhof handed it over to the human race, *la homaro.*

Esperanto in action

The common factors, then, between Esperanto and Basic Income are that each was developed from concern for the worst off but both have the potential to be of incalculable benefit to the rest of us. Just one current example is the small book *ESPERANTO, The New Latin for the Church and for Ecumenism*. This was published first in German, then in Esperanto. Once the Esperanto version was on the Web translations began to spring up in many languages: Hungarian, Italian, Croat, Dutch, Polish. Slovak to begin with. The author, Dr. Ulrich Matthias has much support for his argument that thousands of minority languages are dying, drowned by the surge of powerful commercial languages, especially English and Russian but that this does not bother international business; on the contrary. The EU produces schemes to encourage students to learn the languages of neighbouring countries, but an enquiry found that only about five per cent choose to do so; most wish to learn English. Dr. Matthias says that the Churches – this applies especially to the Catholic Church, which had a worldwide neutral language for fourteen hundred years but allowed it by oversight to melt away – now need to choose whether to accept a method of internal communication that would tend by example to protect the thousands of endangered languages, or do nothing, rely on Italian and some kind of approximate English and let the lesser languages perish.

Wider effects

It is not only the speakers of the lesser-used languages who would benefit from a wide adoption of Esperanto. At present the United Nations and the European Union spend very large sums on translation and interpreting – money which comes from taxes paid by citizens of member countries who do not speak any of the 'working languages' and are therefore doubly penalized. Claude Piron, who had been a polyvalent translator and recorder for the World Health Organization, resigned in 1975 and wrote an open letter to the Director. In his letter he listed a few of the appeals made in that year to the WHO, one to cure trachoma, one for 83,000 dollars to fight leprosy in Burma, one a mere 26,000 dollars for basic hygiene in the Dominican Republic. These and other modest requests had been turned down for lack of funds. But the same Assembly that refused these grants voted five million United States dollars yearly for the purpose of making Chinese and Arabic working languages. He added that the projects for the whole African region amounted to 4,205,442 dollars, a little less than the sum allocated to extra translation. But the combined contributions of the Nordic countries amounted to 3,052,160 dollars; Piron asked, did the citizens of those countries really agree to having the whole of the money they had given being swallowed up by Babel, when so much remains to be done in the world?

Piron advanced a solution which would combine cost effectiveness with linguistic justice. If the assembly would decide that in ten or fifteen years' time Esperanto would be the only language used in meetings and documents it would certainly be found, long before the time was up, that each national delegation would contain several younger members who spoke Esperanto as well as they spoke their mother-tongue. Older members could be expected to have a good passive knowledge; nowadays almost all delegates understand English, French or Spanish. 'It is child's play to move from one ot these languages to understanding of Esperanto'.*Transiri de la kompreno de unu el tiuj lingvoj al la kompreno de Esperanto estas infanlude simpla,* [A few words to display this simplicity: transiri. Trans+ iri; all verbs indicate the infinitive by the ending i; ti + u + j, uj pronounce rather like *oui* in French; lingvo, language + j, lingvoj, plural, oj like -oy in English; nouns end with o; infanlude, child +game, the ending e indicates an adverb. Any root can become a noun, verb, adverb, adjective, by addition of o; as, is, os; e, or a as in *simpla.*]

Help for children

One may say at least that were Esperanto not cold-shouldered, just as Basic Income usually is, it would be doing much good in the world; insofar as it would make funding available for health it would assist children's development. But simply as a language it is even now doing much to help children. Children in countries of the 'developed' world spend many school years being taught foreign languages. They are required to learn idioms, memorise the conjugations of verbs, and take care in most languages to give each noun its proper gender. English is gender-free, but it provides special spelling hazards: where Italian can manage with 28 phonemes, to write it requires 33 graphemes; French is a little more difficult, with 36 phonemes which require 190 graphemes; English can identify 62 phonemes which to be written correctly require 1,120 items of spelling.

Since Esperanto was carefully pruned by its young designer (who had suffered all the pains of learning the languages most commonly taught now as well as Latin, Greek and Hebrew, while Polish was his first language) children who have learnt it easily have been found by much research in many countries to be able attack second and third languages with confidence. This is the same sort of confidence Montessori's materials and affirmation are able to instill. Dr. Claude Piron, who retired recently from his post in the Department of Psychology in the University of Geneva has repeatedly diagnosed a mental illness which he calls the Babel Syndrome:

> Que Babel soit une névrose, nous l'avons vu a plusieurs resprises ... Pensez à tous ces millions d'enfants qui apprennent les langues de par le monde, par un résultat quasi-nul. Pensez à tous ces milliards qu'on dépense pour la traduction et l'interprétation, alors qu'il suffit de regarder comment la communication fonctionne dans une association d'espérantophones pour voir que cela coûte infiniment moins cher d'obtenir un résultat infiniment supérieur....S'il s'agissait, non pas de l'ensemble de la sociéte humaine, mais d'une personne, on dirait q'elle est névrosée pour se debrouiller aussi mal quand l'experience prouve qu'il est si facile se débrouiller aussi bien.

I may not disagree; Piron has much longer and wider experience than I, he has addressed much more eminent audiences, but still I am inclined towards a milder diagnosis. It seems to me that part of the problem is a lack of imagination. Is it not strange that while the idea of unemployment assistance is hardly a century old, there seems to be a widespread conviction that any state subvention really must be conditional? As soon as I read about the National Dividend I remembered how groups of people in ancient Ireland, (we called them Tuath) owned territory in common and shared responsibility. With the Dividend in place, everyone could feel that their ancient aunt, their problem cousin, the child who had airy-fairy notions of being an artist – would never be totally dependent on a single hardworking breadwinner. Young people would not be slaves to examinations. I could also see how jobs that are intrinsically disagreeable might be well paid, how a few people could pool their dividend to set up some novel enterprise, like inventing the Internet, how, especially, everyone would be able to see themselves as respect-worthy citizens, This seems to me so obvious that in this paper I see no need to argue for an adequate Basic Income.

The language picture is similar. Everyone knows that learning languages is, save for a few specially gifted people, a long hard slog. In Ireland this belief is exceptionally pervasive, since so many have spent so many years in situations where there was a pretence that they were being taught Irish, but where the result was, as Piron says, quasi-nul. They cannot imagine a world which would resemble Ivan Illich's picture of the twelfth century philosopher-scientist, Hugh of St. Victor.

Hugh was like a moving flame. Brought up in German, he lived in Paris, but his own language was Latin. This Latin was the kind of language which English speakers today experience great difficuly in understanding. No one was born to it. Scholars learned its classical variety. But for scholars, scribes, religious and lawyers it then became the main language of everyday intercourse. Therefore, they felt entitled to shape it to their needs, their feelings, their whims. It was not a dead language, nor an élite language into which only some are born. It was the living language of a scholarly community, where all who used Latin came to it relatively late in life. It is therefore a kind of tongue our age has lost.

This is the kind of tongue to which I have, relatively late in life at the age of sixty, become accustomed: enjoying a brilliant play about a day in the life of the Empress Maria Theresa, staged in Zagreb with a Bulgarian and Croat cast; in Budapest discussing economics and the Korean alphabet with Professor So Gilsu, Professor of economics in Seoul, during a break in an intensive conference on Transport and the Environment. Unlimited bottles and jugs of Tokay, the Wine of Kings, the King of Wines, brought out from cool caves on a sunbaked Hungarian mountainside. There is so much more than that to be met on the Internet: there is, of course, constant discussion about the language problems of the European Union but also word of festivals in the Ukraine, conferences in Brazil and Sweden, youth having fun in Hungary, people of Togoland teaching Esperanto to refugees from Angola, Iranians teaching Afghans, young Koreans, Japanese and Chinese having yearly peace meetings.

This brings me towards the close. It was a Japanese Deputy Secretary General who believed that a wide adoption of a neutral, easily learnt language would support the ideal of world peace. It was, unfortuntely, the then French Minister for Public Instruction who, confident that French was the proper language for international diplomacy, instructed the French delegates to sideline the Resolution. Dr. Nitobe is reported to have said, 'In twenty years' time they will be laughing at us'. In twenty years time it was 1942 and people were not laughing.

5th perception: The Noosphere

But there were others gifted with imagination as well as intelligence. It was in 1925 that Pierre Teilhard de Chardin coined the word 'noosphere', signifying a new layer or membrane on the earth's surface, a 'thinking layer' superposed on the living layer of the biosphere and the lifeless layer of inorganic material, the lithosphere. True, already at that time telegraph, telephone and radio could enable some people to send some ideas across national barriers. But in 1983, during the Esperanto congress in Budapest, I heard the Secretary-General of the World Telecommunications Union, Mr. Robert Butler, say that the technology for communication was of no use unless the people at either end could understand one another. He added that in five years computers would probably be capable of speech recognition for everyday purposes; when that time came, they would need a more logical language than anything now in use; it was not for him to say whether or not Esperanto might be that language.

He could not foresee that in the intervening twenty years computers would not be laboriously speaking to each other, but would instead be sending millions of messages, letters, documents written in a supra-national language in which writers could not only express simply what they were thinking but spell every word as familiarly as they could spell their own names. A language having, instead of 96 phonemes signified by 1,120 graphemes, a mere 28 of each. A language for the noosphere.

Two final paragraphs from *The Phenomenon of Man*:

> There can be no doubt that, to an imaginary geologist coming one day in the far future to inspect our globe in fossil form, the most astounding of the revolutions undergone by the earth would be that which took place at the beginning of what has so rightly been called the psychozoic era. And even today, to a Martian capable of analysing sidereal radiations psychically no less than physically, the first characteristic of our planet would be, not the blue of the seas or the green of the forests, but the phosphorescence of thought.
>
> The greatest revelation open to science today is to perceive that everything precious, active and progressive originally contained in that cosmic fragment from which our world emerged, is now concentrated in and crowned by the noosphere.

While I copied those paragraphs I thought, surely he wrote that before it had become evident that we could use the power of thought to invent means to destroy both ourselves and other species. No; there is a philosophical appendix on evil in evolution, written in 1948. Fr. Pierre Teilhard de Chardin was Jesuit; his superiors required him to refrain from publication, hence the delay of ten years before the book was published. It had to wait until after his death.

Translucent or Transparent?

Translation into Esperanto Compared to Wrapping in Cling-Film

> Culture may now be said to be the whole complex of distinctive spiritual, material, intellectual and emotional features that characterise a society or social group. It includes not only the arts and letters, but also modes of life, the fundamental rights of the human being, value systems, traditions and beliefs.
>
> (UNESCO World Conference on Cultural Policies, 1982, quoted in Healy & Reynolds, 1996)

It is, perhaps surprising that this definition, no doubt carefully considered, and certainly translated from wherever it originated into five other official languages does not specify language. UNESCO has its own problems. However, arts and letters, intellectual and emotional features are expressed in language; if a society is to conserve and develop its culture the language, or languages, in which they have been expressed must at least not perish. Clearly, it is much to be desired that every language live its natural life, changing organically, borrowing, merging, but not being submerged and lost.

The danger of submersion is not remote or theoretical. I am not referring to the state of affairs in this country, but to a wider screen. Dr. John

Honey is a professor of Teaching English as a Foreign Language; he has worked largely in the East. He believes that English is killing one language a week, worldwide, and for him this is not a cause for concern; it's what people want. I heard him say so, during a debate about Esperanto He was debating with a Welsh academic, Dr. John Wells.

To have English from infancy is good fortune. It has been increasing its territory contemporaneously with moveable type so it enables a vast range of choice. But my concern in this context is that it carries with it so much cultural baggage. For example, it is the language of Ricardo and Adam Smith; the words which give the initials GNP are English words. Almost everyone is familiar with these initials; lately they have been frequent in the press. The assumption normally is that an increase in Gross National Product is a Good Thing. This is the language of the Market Economy. We see what upheaval upon upheaval it has brought to the former USSR and now to China. Because English is perceived as the key to growth and profit, millions want to learn English. There is little or no awareness that a good pile up on a motorway results in a great deal of expensive activity repairing or disposing of people and things, and that every pound spent is a pound gained somewhere and an addition to the GNP.

'Externalities' are the losers; pure air, clean water; some have included women among 'externalities'. Language and culture are at risk. No need to say that Ireland has not escaped. Would a community that remembered how Fionn had tasted the Salmon of Knowledge permit a single salmon to be held in a cage?

But the good news is that there are other ways of measuring true prosperity; there is another way of talking to each other without any intrusion on either language, by either language. In 1887 a young Polish doctor used the dowry of his newly-wed wife, Klara Zilbernik, with the full agreement of herself and her father, to publish a booklet setting out the structure of an international language which would protect the users of less powerful languages against linguistic imperialism. Zamenhof published versions in Russian, Polish, German, French. An Irish linguist, Richard Geoghegan, wrote to him in Latin, and translated the booklet, by 'Dr. Esperanto' into English. The first congress, when 688 people from thirty different countries found they could not only read and write Esperanto but talk and argue and celebrate, was held in France in 1905. Believe me, this is an exhilarating experience – and it is open to anyone who wishes.

The language reached China at about the same time; the first Esperanto organisation there was founded in Shanghai in 1909; by 1912 the Minister for Education proposed it as an option in normal schools. Now, among many other things, there are annual conventions of Chinese, Korean and Japanese young people, speaking Esperanto, of course. Anyone who remembers the Sino-Japanese war or knows how the Japanese in general regard Koreans will recognise the significance of this. The

President of the Universala Esperanto-Asocio, Prof. Lee Chong-Yeong is Korean. Him I have seen only at a distance, at the congress in Finland when he was elected, but another Korean professor of economics, Dr. So Gilsu, a former *estrarano* is genial and energetic. During a conference on Transport and the Environment held in Budapest, having Magyar, Esperanto and English as working languages, he borrowed some time to have a seminar on economics for those interested. This somehow shifted into an exploration of the history and elegance of the Korean alphabet, and of how the school system failed to awaken students to its beauty. I had the good luck to broadcast on Budapest radio along with him; no doubt he could have talked for days, naturally in Esperanto, about anything under the sun.

Dr. So Gilsu was in the Esperanto-speaking audience, some of whom were English, when Prof. John Honey told us that English was what everyone wanted to learn, though most fail. Dr. So took the opportunity to say that he had been learning English for twenty years, but that he did not feel he could stand up in that room and make a statement in English; he went on to make some dry observations about the use of 'East' and 'West', because of course for Koreans the East, the Orient, from whence the sun rises, is North America.

Japanese speakers of Esperanto similarly feel at home in the language. To be an expert magician is respectable; to perform as a laughably inexpert magician is another thing – though it also requires considerable latent skill. It is not something that a cultured Japanese man would be inclined to do before foreigners, but I have enjoyed such a performance before an audience of *samideanoj* (members of a group having similar ideas – esperantists) from various countries. That, I'm almost sure, was a congress in Spain. I am sure that it was in Norway, in Bergen, that another Japanese *samideano*, sitting at the top table, facing the audience, was so touched by the praise given to the friend whose place he was taking for a ceremonial presentation, that he buried his face in his hands and wept. The friend, too shy to come, has devoted himself for many years to searching out and publishing everything Zamenhof wrote (*Iam kompletigota verkaro* – the works, going to be completely collected sometime).

Still in Bergen, I can shift from real life to literature, (though I do not promise that real life will not keep breaking in). The Congress Centre was the Grieghallen, a theatre with a sufficiency of meeting rooms. In this theatre, in Ibsen's home-town, we had a performance of *The Doll's House* convincing enough to raise the blood-pressure of many of the audience. I at least felt much more involved than when I have seen Ibsen played in English; it seems to me that the translator has to choose between contemporary English, which brings the problems of the characters into question, or English as it used to be spoken, which distances the audience,

I have tried to demonstrate that Esperanto enables cultural osmosis, which surely is relevant to 'Culture and language Learning', but naturally our contact with other literatures and cultures is more often through print. I must. then indicate the features of the language that make it peculiarly flexible, able to be moulded to follow the windings of the text being packaged.

First, the system of affixes. Every root can be used as noun, adjective, verb, adverb if this makes sense:esper**o**, hope; esper**a**, an adjective, I suppose, hopeful; mi esper**as**, I hope, vi esper**is**, you hoped, ili esper**os**, they will hope; esper**e**, an adverb, perhaps the intrusive 'hopefully', but more often we say 'esper**eble'** adding **ebl** indicating possibility; *espereble ne pluvos morgau,* there's a good chance it won't rain to-morrow.

The history of the language and of attempts to improve and compete with it, shows that Zamenhof's determination to retain the use of an accusative case was justified; it permits clarity and also considerable liberty in respect of word order. Claude Piron, in *La Bona Ling*vo provides discussion with examples, from which I shall borrow a little. He compares three translations by eminent Esperantists of Verlaine's *Chanson d' Automne* of which I shall quote only one, that by Kalomano Kalocsy, because he is eminent as a poet not only in Esperanto but also in Hungarian.

Les sanglots longs	*La velksezon'*
Des violons	*Per violon'*
De l'automne	*ĝemsona*
Blessent mon coeur	*Vundas ĉe l'kor*
D'une langueur	*Min per langvor'*
Monotone	*Monotona.*

But Piron's theme is essentially the cross-cultural capacity of Esperanto, and he is not satisfied with the intrusion of the word *langvor, langvoro* which does not exist in the ordinary language. He says:

> One must not forget that, to transfer anything from one culture to another, the first condition is to use words that will be understood. The idea that *langvor* is a faithful translation is an illusion; it transfers something only to people for whom it is richly evocative. To feel the harmonics of a word, one must have met it a hundred - or at least fifty -times in different circumstances and contexts. A dictionary definition reaches only, as we have seen, the left half of the brain, which is the half least affected by poetry.

With the experience of having been a translator of several languages for the UN, Esperanto he finds to be, as a *poesiatraduklingo,* superior to any other that he knows. He demonstrates this by producing four other translations of the same verse, with comments. And, while insisting that he is not a poet, he thinks the most faithful, follows:

Singulta son'
De violon'
Velksezona
Min vundas plu
Per kor-enu'
Unatona.

Faithful translation of Latin makes accessible literature that was formerly open to almost all who were able to read; it's pleasant to be able to enjoy Erasmus' *Praise of Folly,* with Holbein's own marginal illustrations. The Latin of the litugy transforms very well indeed. The difficulties that English translators experience – or refuse to acknowledge – with 'man' 'men' and 'brothers' do not arise; *vir* is *viro, homo* is *homo.* It happened that I was offered an opportunity to learn something of New Testament Greek about the time I first met Esperanto. I found that, in the opening verses of St. John's Gospel, with which people of my age are familiar, where we used to hear 'through him all things were made, and without him was made nothing that was made' the Greek text had a verb, *egéneto,* 'came into being'; the Esperanto text matches precisely:*esti,* infinitive, 'to be', + *-iĝ* affix signifying become. *ĉio estiĝis per li, kaj aparte de li estiĝis nenio.*

This affix is in constant use. Hence I feel extra confidence in reading translations of Plato or Aeschylus. Classical studies which are now taught in translation would benefit if some texts were presented in this way. This also may be reciprocal: a group of Esperanto speakers in Italy enjoyed a seminar held in Latin.

My next example comes from a translation that others will be better able to check than I am. I find that it rushes along, fierce and witty. The Scottish printer found that he could understand it, because this, *La Meznokta Kortumo,* The Midnight Court, he refused to print, considering it indecent. Dr.

Goodheir had to send it to a printer in Holland. Liam O Cuirc, who translates from the Irish, knows several English versions and considers this the most faithful. It is worth mentioning that Liam learnt Irish in school, 'did' it in his Leaving Certificate, but felt no particular interest until he learnt Esperanto. Such an effect is not unusual. Indeed, I have compared some verses in *Kings, Lords and Commons* and have noted that Frank O'Connor, in 1961, found it best to be relatively prudish. Here I offer a mere four lines from the opening verses; blue sky, flaming sun setting out from the night avid to run its daily round:

> La ĉielo hieraú frue klaris,
> Suno julia fajre flamis
> ekvojaĝante el la nokto,
> avida por sia taga rondo.

Is it not an aspect of culture and language learning that this poem has been favourably reviewed in a Chinese magazine which is read in a hundred countries? This is reciprocal; any one of the principal Esperanto magazines is likely to have notices of books published in China. I picked one that came to hand; no reviews, but a set of Chinese jokes, collected by Wu Suzhen: A teacher wrote in a student's notebook, 'Little Hong talks too much during lessons'. The girl's father replied, 'If you knew her mother you certainly wouldn't be surprised'.

Exotic culture? But lest it seem that MONATO is a magazine for the simple-minded, it should be mentioned that the same issue reports on the falling birthrate in Lithuania, miserable daily life in Tagisthan. In Madagascar foreign factories employ young people in conditions equivalent to slavery. There also students are suffering the effects of a decision in 1972 to change the language of instruction from French to Malagasay; teachers were then taught only that language; now the Minister for Education has decided to revert to French, but the teachers are naturally unable to comply. Pupils are accustomed only to their native language, so standards are collapsing, in spite of contributions from France. These reports, surely relevant to UNESCO's definition of culture, are sent from Madagascar, where there are some extraordinarily devoted *samideanoj,*

The last paragraph intruded; my intention was to say something about Chinese poetry in Esperanto. The collection translated by Professor S. J. Zee begins with poems from the *Libro de Poezio,* compiled in the fifth century BC, which were looked on as models by subsequent poets. Nature, peace, home and family affection are frequent themes; war is detested. That which I quote is a typical complaint of a wife whose husband is far off, probably on military service; days and months have passed; when shall we see each other! Under the rays of the setting sun the sheep and cattle are going into their shelters. My beloved is far, God save him from hunger and thirst!

> Mia kara estas for,
> Pasis tagoj kaj monatoj.
> Kiam ni revidos nin, amato!
> Kokoj jam ripozis sur sidstango,

Sub la kliniĝantaj sunradioj
Ŝafoj kaj bovoj enstaliĝas ankaŭ
Mia kara estas for,
Dio lin gardu de soifo kaj malsato!

In his introduction Professor Zee provides a history of Chinese poetry and and a summary of the metric system, based on two-syllable feet. Classical Chinese is, he says, much more concise than Esperanto, 'so one constantly finds oneself being left behind in the race and even having to double the length of the verses'. On which my comment is that Esperanto is notably more concise than the widely used European languages, while his collection is so pleasing that I needed an hour to make a choice. There is two way traffic; the current catalogue lists *Poemoj el Fremdlando,* original and translated poems in Esperanto, with Chinese translation. Indeed, the language has enabled translation of a considerable quantity of European literature into Chinese.

Korea, Japan, China; Ireland, Norway, Madagascar; French, Latin and Greek; I have in passing mentioned Polish, Russian and Italian. That current catalogue lists children's stories from Sweden, Lithuania, Cuba, from Israel and from Croatia. In fiction, there's an anthology of modern short stories from Bosnia-Herzegovina, in translation. Among novels and autobiographies written in Esperanto there's an adventurous Argentinian, a Jew living undercover in Budapest during the last war, an Italian detective having a hard time between his mother and his girlfriend while hunting terrorists (to whom did I lend it?) a series of convincing detective stories by Istvan Nemere, who writes best-sellers in Hungarian as well. Translations are far too many to be listed here, but perhaps three stories of contemporary Vietnam, a novel from Japan about the inundation of Gulu in 1109, and life in Bengal in the thirties and forties from the point of view of an independent young woman, suggest possibilities of cultural exploration, especially remembering that they are translated into the international language by native speakers of that in which they were written.

Pray remember, translation is normally from a learnt language into the mother tongue of the translator. Even if the translator is truly bilingual, he or she must aim to produce something that conforms to the style of the target language. Esperanto is different; it's one's own language; feel free to play with it, as Zamenhof invited us to – just keeping his sixteen rules.

Finally a two thousand year old song from China, the song of an elerly person who gets out of bed at daybreak, reposes when the sun goes down, ploughs for his food, dug a well to drink from:

> Mi ellitiĝas ĉe l'tagiĝo
> Kaj ĉe la sunsubir' mi ripozas:
> Teron mi plugas por min nutri,
> Por trinki mi mem puton fosas:
> Kion mi devas danki al la suvereno !

What am I supposed to thank the government for?

SEPTEMBER 1922:
WHAT MIGHT HAVE BEEN

Before the beginning of this book, on the 31 August 1921, Dr. Nitobe Inazou, Assistant Secretary General of the League of Nations, presented to the Secretary-General his report, following his observation of the 13th World Esperanto Congress in Prague.The result of this report was research which in the following year persuaded the Assembly of the League to recommend to all members that they should gradually introduce in their primary schools the teaching of Esperanto, and that they should inform the League of Nations of the steps they had taken.

31 August is the day before 1 September; it was on that day in 1921 I was born.

I had not heard anything about Dr. Nitobe until his report was published in 1998 in a tri-lingual book, *Al lingva demokratio. Towards Linguistic Democracy. Vers la démocratie linguistique.*

It has been well said that this remarkably objective report failed to change the face of the world but that indeed it almost succeeded. *en septembre 1922, il présentait un rapport remarquablement objectif qui a failli changer la face du monde. A vrai dire,il s'en est fallu de très grand peu ...*

'Almost succeeded'. Should I have said, 'a near thing' or 'touch and go'? Claude Piron's original French is there as an apt example of how much is lost in translation; English cannot accept 'it failed in this by a very large/great little ...' The inadequacy of translation is one of the arguments in support of Esperanto, but it is not the most significant.

The Report to which Piron refers is that made in 1922, in the Palace of the League of Nations, entitled *International Conference on Esperanto in Schools*. Hundreds of teachers and professors from 28 countries took part. It was, of course, prompted by Dr. Nitobe's proposal of investigation. Here are its conclusions from experience in 250 cities throughout the world:

> 1. Teaching of Esperanto helps children to have a deeper understanding of their own languages.
>
> 2. As a first foreign language, Esperanto is easily learnt. Therefore, having succeeded with the first, the student can approach the second with experience and courage. Rather than being a waste of time, study of Esperanto saves time in the study of foreign languages.
>
> 3. Esperanto assists the study of geography and of peace education. The student learns of the need to accept other cultures.

Those conclusions come from a brief, witty contribution (in Esperanto) by KOBAYASHI Tsukasa to the book mentioned above. Among other things he says that the official languages of the UN are too difficult for ordinary Asians and Africans, while few Europeans want to learn 3,000

Chinese ideograms. But, he adds, we need not insist that Esperanto become an official UN language; ask a group of UN officials whether they drink CocaCola and several will say 'yes', even though it has never been declared to be an official UN drink.

His concern is that Esperanto should be an inter-people language rather than 'inter-national'. Education needs to be life-long, accessible to everyone, at all times and everywhere: *'al ĉiu, ĉiam kaj ĉie.'* We are living longer; older people need to know about major world problems and share in solving them.

Further, he says 'we should look at the psychological problem. Many people, especially the elderly and 19 million refugees, cease to have an aim in life. In Japanese the word *ikigai* is used to indicate an aim in life or a sense that life is worth living. To restore *ikigai* Esperanto is certainly useful, since we have seen many people who gained *ikigai* through Esperanto, for example s-ro AKIGITA Ujaku (1883-1962) a famous dramatist who, having found esperanto, gave up his intention of suicide.

That is the message of a present-day Japanese esperantist. In the past and in this millenium Japanese have made very great contributions to the esperanto movement, so many that if I were to mention them I would be deflected from my purpose, which is to look further at Dr. Nitobe's own report. The more interesting it is, the more depressing I find it; it seems that at that time the seed-bed was large, warm, moist and fertile; young plants were springing up, sheltered by clumps of stronger growth which had survived hard weather. Then fell a lethal frost from France.

Esperanto speakers from 36 countries took part in the 1921 Prague Congess, altogether 2557 people. Dr. Nitobe noted an interesting social mix of teachers, skilled workmen, students and professors, journalists and artists, clergymen and engineers. Nearly 40 per cent were women. He was impressed by the intelligence of the participants and also by their harmony and zeal.

I am impressed by the information that nine governments sent official delegates. What makes me unhappy are Dr. Nitobe's matter of fact references to the report of a Commission on the teaching of modern languages in Britain that 'it might be worth the while of the government, in concert with our Allies, to appoint a Committee to enquire into the potentialites of artificial languages such as Esperanto and its rivals'. Then he writes, 'Numerous documents have reached the Secretariat from important bodies in different countries urging the League of Nations to consider the question of an international language'. He notes the increasing support for an auxiliary language among smaller nationalities: 'Finland voted 25,000 marks to subsidise the Esperanto cause; in Czecho-Slovakia it is an optional subject in schools. The wide interest taken by the Swiss in Esperanto is too well known to repeat'.

He turns to the world of business, observing that it is a truism that for purposes of trade a common language is indispensable and that a number of Chambers of Commerce recommend the teaching of an artificial language. Nitobe's following sentence is as fine an example as I have seen of the third definition of 'irony' in the Shorter OED: 'A discrepancy between the expected and the actual state of affairs'. He wrote:

> A notable case took place in February of the present year (1921), when the Chamber of Commerce of Paris, after careful comparison of Esperanto with French (to see if the former can convey the precision of the latter), decided to introduce optional instruction in Esperanto in all its commercial schools and to recommend to the Chambers of Commerce in all countries that they should afford facilities for commercial transactions by a rapid propagation of an auxiliary language'.

The expected state of affairs was clearly a picture of rapid progress and co-operation. The actual state of affairs turned out to be skilful, intentional torpedoing of the Esperanto enterprise by the French Minister for Public Instruction. Léon Bérard. He had just forbidden the teaching of Esperanto or propaganda for it in all French schools; 'it was a dangerous tool of internationalism and would be a rival to the French language'.

I have beside me a whole chapter recounting the arguments made in the first Committee in the course of seven meetings, followed by some account of the Commission for Intellectual Co-operation to which French pressure had contrived to pass the parcel. This Commission had been set up to organise universities; some members said this was not a matter they could decide in one morning and that they could not judge a language they did not know. But the famous philosopher Bergson was president of the Commission and he had been instructed by Bérard to 'drown the push for Esperanto'.

It is distressing to remember that Bergson himself had long had a positive view of the language, as had Senator Reynald, who had been head of the earlier French delegation. Most of the members even of the Intellectual Co-operaton commission thought well of it, though one or two preferred Latin. But the two Presidents followed orders; they recommended that the League should wait and see, meanwhile recommending study of foreign languages.

In 1924 the General Assembly of the League voted to accept this resolution. All were aware that it was a political decision. France was a Great Power. It is interesting to note that Chna, Japan, Persia, Britain always supported Esperanto

When asked, Dr. Nitobe said that in twenty years' time the commission would be laughed at. In twenty years time 1944 had arrived.

This this 'treason of the clerks' may not have been such a catastrophe as the burning of the Library of Alexandria or the endless broken treaties with Native Americans or the destruction of centuries old terrace cultivation.

It goes without saying that it has none of the horror of the Holocaust. But it should be remembered that thousands of the victims of Stalin and Hitler (including St. Maximilian Kolbe) perished because they were associated with the idea of world-peace and a language for everyone.

I do not think it beyond argument that if the League had used and supported this well timed language, and the the language, already spread over the globe, had given the advantage of communication to the League, the world's post-war hopefulness might have survived and the Holocaust might never have been dreamt of.

When the official enquiry was opened, in April 1922 the General Secretary of the League, Sir Eric Drummond, observed that the idealistic aim of teachers of Esperanto was similar to the aims of the League of Nations. When, after many debates, the 'Report of the League of Nations on '*Esperanto as a helpful World-language* was published it was an outstanding success. Three editions, in English and French, were sold out in a few months. It was promptly translated into Spanish, Italian, German, Portuguese, Finnish, Hungarian. Japanese, Roumanian and other languages. It was even compatible with the wish for national independence; several of the signatories of the Irish Declaration, including Connolly and Plunkett, either spoke Esperanto or supported it, while they lived.

What happened? Another kind of politics took over. When I was seventeen German youths in brown shirts were singing Deutschland über Alles, Italians, *'Giovannessa, giovanessa, primavera de bellessa,'* and drilling with wooden rifles, French children were still singing that *Enfants de la patrie* should be watering the furrows with impure blood. And three days after my eighteenth birthday Hitler invaded Poland, having given explicit instructions that the family of Zamenhof should be eliminated.

REFERENCES

Comrie, B. (1981) *Universals and Linguistic Typology*

Chomsky, N. (1979) *Language and Responsibility* Harvester.

Comrie, B (1979) *Language Universals and Linguistic Typology* Blackwell, Oxford.

Eco, Umberto (1993) *La Serĉado de la Perfekta Lingvo* Edistudio.

Ertl, l. (1984) Eco kaj Piron; gravaj referencoj. Esperanto 41; 60. UEA, Rotterdam.

Europa Dokumentato 1983 (40-1983) L'esperanto pour mieux apprendre l'anglais.

Fillmore, C (1968) 'The Case for Case' in Back, Emmon & Harms, Robert T., (eds) *Universals in Linguistic Theory* Holt, Rinehart & Winston, New York pp 1-88

Fillmore, C (1977) 'The Case for Case Re-opened'. In *Syntax & Semantics, vol 8* ed. Cole, P & Sadok, M.

Foster, P. (1982) *The Esperanto Movement.* Mouton, The Hague,

Gilbert, W. (1977) *Planlingvaj problemoj.* Stafeto, Kopenhago.

Goodheir, Albert *La Meznokta kortumo,* Vulpo-libroj, Pilger, Laylstad, Nederlando.

Korytkowski, J. (1976). Internacia Lingvo en Eklezio kaj Mondo. Rome. IKUE.

Lins, U. (1988). *La Dangera Lingvo,* pp 385-388. Gerlingen IMoscow: Bleicher Verlag. (also pub in German.)

Matthias, U. (2002), *Esperanto, the New Latin for the Church and for Ecumenism* FEL Antwerp [trans. from German]

Mullarney, M. (1987). The Departure of Latin. *Language Problems and Language Planning* pp. 356-359. Austin TX. University of Texas Press.

(1989). *Esperanto for Hope*, Dublin: Poolbeg.

(1999) *Everyone's Own Language.* Nitobe Press. Dublin

Picasso, M. (1993) La declaracio de Santiago. Literatura Foiro 252.

Piron, C. (1984) *La bona lingvo,* FEL

(1994) Le Defi des Langues: du gâchis au bon sens. Paris. L'Harmattan.

Phillipson, R (2002) *English-Only Europe?* Routledge

Roget, P. *Thesaurus of English Words and Phrases.* 1852 and any subsequent edition.

Rokicki, R. (1987) Leksemstrukturaj aspektoj klasifiki la E. morfemaron, in *Etudes sur la langue internationale.* AIMAV, Gent.

Seppik, Henrik (1971) *La Tuta Esperanto.* Bulgara Esperantista Asocio. Sofia.

Seppik, H., (1987) *La tuta Esperanto,* Hungara Esperanto-Asocio, Budapest.

Symoens, E. (1991) La profedeutica Valoro de Esperanto Rotterdam, C.E.D.

Wells, J. C. (1969) Concise Esperanto and English Dictionary. Hodder and Stoughton., London.

Wells, J.C. (1978) Lingvistikaj aspektoj de Esperanto, UEA, Rotterdam

Zee, S. J. *Libro de Poesio.* Fremdlingva Eldonejo, Beijing.

Al lingva demokratio/ Towards Linguistic Democracy/ Vers la démocratie linguistique. Aktoj de la Nitobe-Simpozio de Internaciaj Organizaĵoj. Rotterdam: UEA 1998

APPENDIX:

In ending these arguments about language, it is appropriate to reflect on the economy and clarity of this letter, published in the review ESPERANTO, and translated for the present reader into English:

> Now 88 years of age, I have for 70 years read every page of the review *Esperanto.* I would like, at the end of my life, to have others, just once, read my words.
>
> People have rights: that is the essence of democracy. No one should be discriminated against because of their skin colour, nationality, religion or anything else. Language also, part of each one's unique culture, has its own rights. Some languages should not be humiliated while others are privileged. It is wrong, for example, that only English speakers should be promoted in the civil service or that French must be used in international affairs or that police should ignore requests from anyone who does not speak Japanese.
>
> In Japan, a little over a hundred years ago, the Meiji-Restoration government decided, on account of opening up the country to the outside world, to regulate the Japanese language and teach it in official schools, to be used throughout the country. Soon Japanese

began to be used countrywide alongside the graceful local speech.

Similarly, Esperanto will come to be used as a bridge between people alongside their local national languages.

Some people fantasize that English should be the second language in Japan. Absurd. Japanese in its own territory and Esperanto worldwide – that's plenty.

Let everybody's native language and Esperanto provide together for world communication. Anyone who wishes may learn whatever other languages they choose, according to their liking or their needs.

OKAMURA RINZÓ -JAPANIO (Ŧ)

Esperanto, a language of hope, a language of peace, the language for all.